# DRESSAGE
# SOLUTIONS

# DRESSAGE SOLUTIONS

## *A Rider's Guide*

### ARTHUR KOTTAS-HELDENBERG

with Andrew Fitzpatrick

KENILWORTH PRESS

First published in the UK in 2014
by Kenilworth Press, an imprint of Quiller Publishing Ltd

British Library Cataloguing-in-Publication Data
A catalogue record for this book is available from the British Library

ISBN 978-1-905693-82-5

Design and typesetting by Paul Saunders

**Photographs by Ewald Willibald**
(except those from the collection of Arthur Kottas-Heldenberg on pages 8 and 11)
**Drawings by Dianne Breeze**

Printed in China

## Kenilworth Press

An imprint of Quiller Publishing Ltd
Wykey House, Wykey, Shrewsbury, SY4 1JA
Tel: 01939 261616 Fax: 01939 261606
E-mail: info@quillerbooks.com
Website: www.quillerpublishing.com

# CONTENTS

# ACKNOWLEDGEMENTS

The authors would like to thank Caroline and Patricia Kottas-Heldenberg for their time and expertise in modelling throughout this book for Ewald Willibald's excellent photographs.

We would also like to express our gratitude to Dianne Breeze for her hard work in producing the outstanding artwork and to Fiona Passey D.O., N.D. for her advice on suitable human stretching exercises.

A great debt of thanks to Alex and Nick Cookson and the Training the Teachers Tomorrow Trust, for allowing us to meet at their home and discuss the book and for all their encouragement and support during this project.

Thanks also to the riders and horses of the Classical Riding School, Lipica Stud Farm, Slovenia, for allowing us to show their superb High School work and again to Ewald Wilibald for taking the photographs.

We would also like to acknowledge the continued help and encouragement of John Beaton of Kenilworth Press, the design skills of Paul Saunders and Martin Diggle for proof reading the manuscript.

## Illustrations

All photographs are reproduced by permission of the photographer Ewald Willibald with the exception of those on pages 8 and 11 which are from the collection of Arthur Kottas-Heldenberg.

All drawings are reproduced by permission of the artist Dianne Breeze.

*above* Arthur Kottas showing an affinity with animals at a very young age!

*above* Arthur Kottas as a boy showing the early stages of the correct seat.

*left* Competitions were a regular part of childhood.

# INTRODUCTION

This book offers advice on day-to-day training problems within the framework of Classical training. It is designed so that readers can refer easily to a common problem, discover the reasons behind it and find some solutions. Obviously not every instance can be covered, but it is hoped that it will provide a resource that will be of use to instructors and riders alike.

A problem-solving book needs to place those solutions in context, so it is necessary to outline correct practice, for without structure, training cannot develop smoothly. It has been said that it takes two lifetimes to learn how to ride; *Dressage Solutions* is offered as a guide along the way.

All the advice contained in this volume is based on sound Classical principles of training and has been proven in everyday situations. These principles always have the horse's welfare and comfort at heart and seek to work with the horse, not against him. There are no 'quick fixes' to be found in the philosophy of correct training, but rather it is a case of logical progression within a system proven to work for thousands of horses over hundreds of years.

*These principles always have the horse's welfare and comfort at heart ...*

At first glance, a way of riding that requires hard work, patience and understanding of your equine partner, may seem unappealing in today's world where instant success is often the unrealistic expectation. However, the rewards of pursuing the Classical way of training are great. We should not forget that we ask the horse to work for us, and if we do it right, he can be a willing partner and friend.

Good riders treat the horse with respect; there should be trust between them. We have to learn how the horse sees the world and behave accordingly. This does not mean attributing human qualities to our horse, but rather to act with patience, calmness and kindness whenever we are with him.

When riding, we communicate with our horse through a language of touches and pressures from our legs, seat and reins and we must be consistent in our aiding. If we do not follow a clear system, he will not understand. When this happens, problems can develop as the horse becomes confused, frustrated or anxious. Our job is to help him understand and to have confidence in his human companion.

Readers will notice the emphasis on the need to develop a correct seat and although this can take time, once attained, the rider can become a positive influence in the horse's training. This should be the aspiration of every rider, whether they wish to compete, or just enjoy the satisfaction of educating a horse to high levels. Our aim is to improve the lot of our horse whether he is an equine superstar or not. Both are equally deserving of good treatment and training.

This book is presented in easy to use sections; beginning with an explanation of the seat, followed by an examination of the gaits, basic training, and lateral work and on up to more advanced work.

In most cases a 'blueprint' (see Glossary) will be offered as a good example. Then common faults will be outlined and the reasons why they are important, before offering solutions. Where the problems discussed originate in the seat, to avoid repetition and where appropriate, the reader is asked to refer back to the relevant points in the chapter on the seat.

> *Our aim is to improve the lot of our horse whether he is an equine superstar or not.*

Before joining the Spanish Riding School, Arthur rode in many show jumping competitions.

It is hoped that both riders and their instructors will find this volume helpful. As ever, there is nothing new in riding; but learning to ride well is about communication and understanding. We hope that this new book can offer some insights to give you and your horse fun when you ride.

*right* Early days at the Spanish Riding School.

*below left* Riding piaffe in the Winter Riding School, Vienna.

*below right* Horse and rider showing great concentration during a performance of the Spanish Riding School.

# GENERAL THOUGHTS

## BE FIT TO RIDE

Dressage riding requires both mental focus and a degree of physical fitness. If we are flexible in our own muscles and joints and have reasonable stamina, then we can ride without hindering our horse's way of going.

Some aspects of the seat are developmental. For example, it takes time and practice to attain the desired muscle tone in the lower back and abdomen to be able to make effective seat aids; likewise it is usually necessary to work at stretching the thigh muscles until they can maintain the position required for a deep seat.

However, other aspects of the seat just need to be learned and maintained. Keeping the head up, or holding the reins with the thumbs uppermost, are good habits that are formed by having the self-discipline to make corrections whenever necessary.

Lunge lessons allow the rider to concentrate on developing flexibility and balance, besides learning the basic skills of aiding, without confusing the horse. Gradually the rider will find he can concentrate less on maintaining his own posture and rather more on how the horse is feeling, through his responses to the aids.

Many riders hold office jobs or perhaps have a long drive to the stables, meaning they do not arrive in the best condition to ride. We acknowledge the importance of warming up our horse, but we too should be loose and relaxed. This may not be easy after a stressful day at work, so some stretching exercises for ourselves would be beneficial before we ride.

> *Dressage riding requires both mental focus and a degree of physical fitness.*

*opposite page*
Arthur and Caroline.

There are many ways in which lack of fitness can affect how we ride, for example:

- Tension in our neck and shoulders affects the rein contact.

- A stiff lower back can cause uncomfortable bumping on the horse's back and can ruin the connection from hock to bridle.

- Stiffness in our joints can inhibit the rider's ability to achieve harmony and a deep, adhesive seat.

## Streching exercises

Illustrated opposite are some suggested stretching exercises.

Do not overstretch and hold only as long as feels comfortable to you. *Consult your own physician if you have any concerns before trying any of them.*

Spend around 4 to 5 minutes in total.

1. Begin with 30 seconds of relaxing.

2. Stretching knees up to stomach, 15 seconds for each.

3. Shoulder blade pinch, two times, 8 seconds each.

4. Flatten lower back two times, 10 seconds each.

5. With hands clasped behind your head, curl upwards three times, holding each for 5 seconds.

6. 30 seconds each side.

7. Rest for 30 seconds.

8. 20 seconds each side.

9. Lie flat on your back and stretch arms out and toes down, two times, 5 seconds each.

10. Raise your head and knees up and, with hands clasped around your knees, rock gently for 25 seconds.

11. Finally rest, and allow the stretches to take effect.

## STRETCHING EXERCISES FOR RIDERS

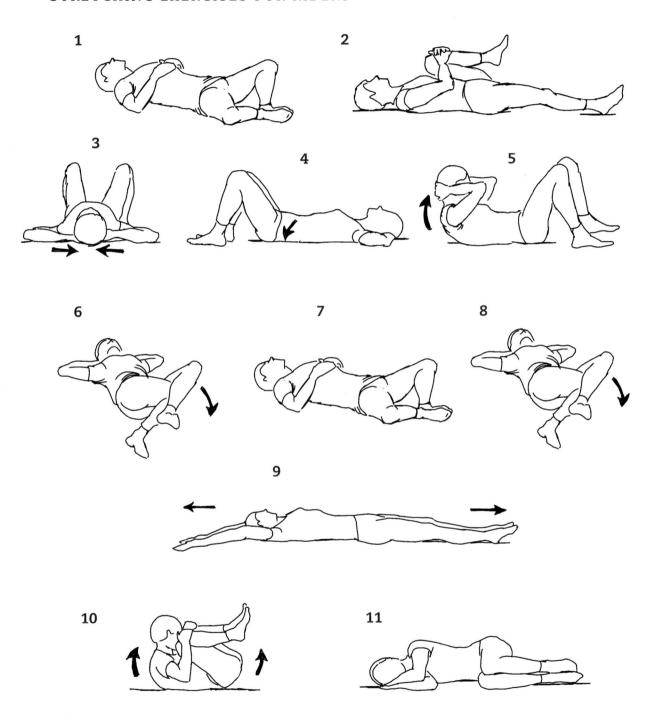

These exercises are good for relieving muscle pain in the lower back, as well as tension in neck and shoulder areas. Ideally do them every night before sleep.

## 2

# THE SEAT

The basis of all good riding is a correct seat. This is essential if the rider is to be balanced and able to communicate effectively with the horse.

Although it takes time and effort to perfect, there is nothing mysterious about the Classical seat. Both functional and elegant, it has been found over centuries to be the most effective, secure and least tiring posture for both horse and rider.

Ideally, acquiring a correct seat should begin with lunge lessons. An experienced trainer should select a steady horse of an appropriate size that will work quietly in a safe arena. These details are important for the safety of all concerned; we should never forget that no matter how calm the horse is, he is not a machine and can be startled.

The lunge lesson should promote confidence and relaxation in the novice rider, making learning an enjoyable experience.

## POSTURE IN THE SADDLE

It is essential to have experienced help from the ground to establish a correct seat, although an important aspect in the rider's training is developing self-awareness, so that a degree of self correction may be made.

This allows the rider to become less dependent on the Trainer for directing every moment of a session, so he can gradually assume more responsibility under the trainer's overall supervision.

When considering the seat position, it will help to have a 'blueprint' in mind, to set an ideal standard.

# THE BLUEPRINT

Achieving the correct seat starts with sitting in the deepest part of the saddle, with the upper body tall and straight. The pelvis should be upright, not tilting forwards, nor collapsed back into a 'chair' seat, which prevents the rider from following the movement of the horse or the effective use of the seat aids.

With equal weight on both seat bones, the coccyx (tailbone) should rest lightly in the saddle. This provides a three-point seat, akin to sitting on a three-legged stool, which allows for a secure and balanced posture in the saddle.

The upper body should be vertical and not lean to either side.

The head should be held so that the rider looks forwards between the horse's ears. The chin should be up and back and the rider's own ears should be carried level, not tipped down to one side.

The shoulder-blades should be flattened across the back, as if they were being pressed towards each other. This helps to lift the ribcage up from the abdomen and makes it possible to effectively use the seat and back aids when required. The muscles of the abdomen and lower back should show tone without tension, to maintain flexibility and suppleness.

The upper arms should rest on the rider's sides, with the elbows in contact with the body, in the area between the top of the hip bone and the bottom ribs.

There ought to be a clear bend at the elbow joint, which absorbs movement and promotes still hands. The forearms and hands also should be relaxed with no stiffness or rigid joints.

The two hands are carried just above the withers, the left thumb pointing towards the horse's right ear and the right thumb towards the left ear. The fingers will make a fist around the reins, with the finger nails forming a line across the palm. The hands should be upright, as if carrying a wine glass!

The rider's legs drape around the horse's ribcage, with the inside of the thigh muscle flat to the saddle, but not gripping.

The knee cap and toes should point forwards rather than outwards. This allows the leg joints to retain their suppleness, which would be lost if they were twisted out of alignment or braced in position.

The inside of the calves remain in light contact with the horse's sides, offering support and security to the horse.

Like shock absorbers on a car, the ankle joints should be springy to reduce the 'bouncy' quality of a horse in trot or canter.

The heels are the lowest point of the rider, toning the calf muscles and enabling a positive leg aid when necessary.

> *The hands should be upright, as if carrying a wine glass!*

Patricia shows a correct seat; an upright pelvis is essential, as the rest of the position is built on this. The arms show a clear bend at the elbow and the hands are carried in front of the pommel and slightly above the withers. The rider looks up and ahead, whilst the leg drapes close to the horse, but without gripping.

The correct leg position allows the rider's weight to sink down into the saddle and heels, fostering the feeling of being able to sit *inside* the horse's movement, rather than perching on the saddle.

Viewed from the side, there should be a vertical line linking the rider's ear, shoulder, elbow, hip and heel.

This alignment provides stability and, coupled with flexibility in the lower back and all the main joints of the body, allows us to harmonise with the horse's movement, creating a still rider.

The goal is to achieve a balanced, relaxed position that can be maintained without excessive physical effort.

A novice rider may feel that it requires a *good deal of effort* to keep this ideal posture; but like most things worth doing, it takes a little time to get to the stage where a good seat position is second nature.

## THE FUNCTION OF THE SEAT

The seat has three areas of influence in riding.

1. To harmonise (that is, approve or agree) with the way the horse is moving.

2. To contain the horse's speed and length of stride.

3. To lengthen the horse's stride.

> It is important to note that the seat is used as part of the whole aiding system, in conjunction with the legs and reins.

To harmonise with the horse's movement means that the rider's pelvis moves neither more nor less than the horse's stride, but exactly the same. This conveys to the horse that he agrees with the tempo and length of stride. The horse and rider should be seamless in their connection, like having a second skin.

The seat should be used in containing mode, in conjunction with the other aids, when the rider makes a downward transition, or wishes to slow down.

The normal sequence is first apply the legs, then seat and lastly the reins. However, if the horse is strong, it is wise to use the seat first to keep control, then legs, then reins. Note that the reins are always used after the other aids.

During a transition, the rider closes his legs onto the horse to activate the hind legs, encouraging the horse to lift his ribcage and back and tilting the angle of his pelvis. This closes the hind legs further under his belly into a position where they can carry more weight.

As the leg aids take effect, the rider applies the seat aid. A novice or untrained horse may take longer to understand and react to the aids, creating a slight delay before the seat is used; however, with a trained horse who is 'on the aids' the seat, leg and reins may be used almost simultaneously, producing a much quicker reaction.

The technique is for the rider to grow taller in the upper body, lifting the collarbones upwards, simultaneously pressing the elbows down towards the hip bones. This firms the torso, so the horse, feeling the resistance from the rider's pelvis, slows down, seeking the rider's approval through the harmonising seat as noted above.

Do not draw the elbows backwards, as this would pull on the horse's mouth.

Be careful not to brace the back rigidly, as this causes a hollow in the small of the back and tilts the pelvis forward. The back then cannot follow the movement, leading to bouncing in the saddle and soreness for both horse and rider.

As the seat and leg aids take effect, the rider can make soft half-halts along the outside rein. This is delivered by vibrating the rein, not pulling it backwards. This vibration commonly lasts three or four seconds; less if the horse responds sooner.

The 'driving' seat is used, in conjunction with the other aids, to encourage a longer stride, for example, when the rider wishes to ride from working trot to medium. The leg aids prompt the haunches. When the rider feels the horse ready to give more power, his seat makes a longer swing in the saddle, as if making space for the hind legs to make greater ground-gaining steps.

Take care not to grind the seat into the saddle, as this can lead to the horse hollowing his back downwards to avoid the uncomfortable feeling, with a consequent loss of balance and suspension and resulting in running steps and an unhappy horse.

**To summarise:** the rider needs to develop the ability to alter the tone of the torso muscles at will, so that the seat can be used to harmonise, to restrain or to increase the stride.

# WEIGHT AIDS

*… our weight in the saddle can influence direction in a positive or negative way.*

Put simply, our weight in the saddle can influence direction in a positive or negative way. A horse feels comfortable when he is under the centre of our two seat bones. This makes it easier for him to carry us and retain his balance. We can use this to help when turning, circling or when riding lateral movements. When we turn our shoulders to be parallel with the horse's shoulders and move our outside leg behind the girth, it puts more weight onto our inside seat bone. This encourages the horse to move in this direction as he seeks to stay under the centre of our weight.

For example, in travers, renvers or half-pass, when we look in the direction of travel with more weight on the inside seat bone and stirrup, it helps the horse to move smoothly. However, if our weight is on the wrong seat bone, it hampers his movement and rhythm will be affected.

The use of the weight aid should be subtle; a slight adjustment of our weight is all that is needed. If we make big movements it only disturbs the horse.

# POSTURAL FAULTS

## 1. Looking down

This leads to weight being shifted forward and out of the saddle, unbalancing both horse and rider. It can also lead to tension in the neck and shoulders as the body tries to stabilise an unbalanced head position and this tension will be transmitted down the reins to the horse's mouth, leading to contact problems.

The rider must take responsibility and keep the head up!

## 2. Rounded shoulders

This can cause unsteady arms and lead to contact problems.

The rider can use exercises to achieve flattened shoulder blades. Extend a straight arm vertically, and then slowly rotate it backwards, brushing past your ear until you feel the shoulder blade move. At that point, bring the arm down by your side, bend the elbow and bring the fist into position over the withers. This will correct the fault.

This also helps with elbows that turn out.

## 3. Straight arms

Straight arms mean the hands will bounce and disturb the rein contact, possibly hurting the horse's mouth.

Keep a soft bend at the elbow, to absorb the horse's movement. Good hands are harmonious; they move neither more nor less than the horse's head and neck.

See illustration overleaf.

*Keep a soft bend at the elbow, to absorb the horse's movement.*

## 4. Rounded wrists

This will fix the hands, giving a harsh feeling along the reins, leading to the horse bracing his jaw or opening his mouth.

The wrists need to be relaxed, but not limp, so they can make a vibration down the reins during half-halts. This must happen over the withers, not be pulled back behind them.

A rider who fixes his hands/wrists may be out of balance and using his hands for support. This must be corrected by basic work on the ability to sit and follow the horse's movement independently of the reins.

See illustration overleaf.

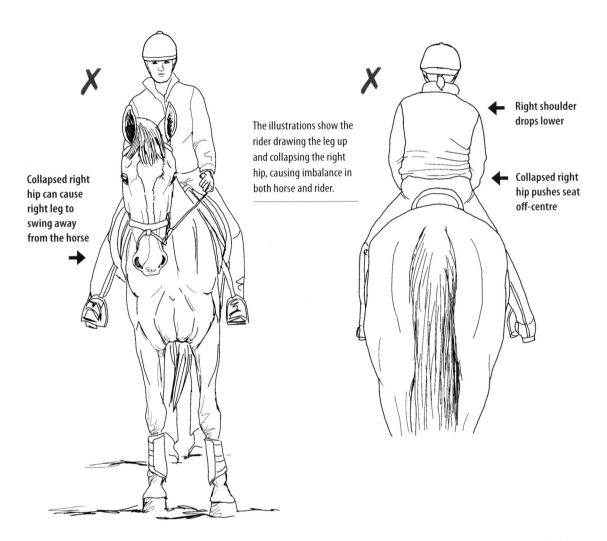

Collapsed right hip can cause right leg to swing away from the horse

The illustrations show the rider drawing the leg up and collapsing the right hip, causing imbalance in both horse and rider.

Right shoulder drops lower

Collapsed right hip pushes seat off-centre

A further cause is when the leg is drawn upwards when giving an aid. This can lead to a hip collapsing. The heel must stay deep when the lower leg pushes the horse. Stretch the leg down after giving an aid to avoid this problem.

## 10. Knees gripping

A rider out of balance often grips with the knees to provide security. Leaning forwards or a stiff lower back can both contribute to the problem. The solution is to work on achieving a deep, independent seat.

The pelvis must be able to follow the horse's movement with a rhythmic, forward swing. Working without stirrups on the lunge is helpful and the rider may be allowed to hold the pommel with one hand to stabilise balance and build confidence.

## 11. Heels up

Both heels should be lower than the toes, with supple ankles. This allows the rider to sit securely into the horse rather than perch in the saddle. Raised heels often mean the calf muscles are slack, leading to ineffective aids.

Check that the stirrups are not too long. Over-long leathers do not make a dressage seat!

Tipping the upper body forwards can sometimes be the root of the problem. Ensure the torso is vertical in the saddle.

Educate the leg to make aids with a flexed calf, not by scraping the heel upwards.

CHAPTER

# 3

# THE BASIC PACES

## WALK

### General remarks

- The walk is a pace of four, regular beats. It should show energy, but not be hurried or tense.

- There is no moment of suspension.

- Free walk on a long rein, medium, collected and extended are the variations recognised.

- In basic training only the free walk and medium walk, are used.

- Collected and extended walk can be difficult to train and so are not used in basic training.

### Free walk

- In the free walk on a long rein, the horse stretches his head and neck longer and lower, maintaining a light contact with the bit. (In a free walk on a *loose* rein, there is no contact with the mouth.)

- The aim is to encourage relaxation so the horse stretches his body and lengthens the steps to the maximum.

- Normally one would want an overtrack of at least two shoes beyond the front hoofprint.

- We use the free walk to loosen the horse's muscles and joints and to encourage the blood circulation around his body before starting his training and during a session as a reward for work well done.

- At the end of his work session, the free walk is used as part of the 'cooling down' so that the horse finishes in a relaxed state and returns to the stable cool, dry, and relaxed.

A good example of relaxation in free walk. The neck stretches forwards and downwards when the reins are offered, and the softly moving ears show a calm horse.

## Medium walk

- The medium walk should have a regular, unhurried quality to the steps.

- The horse should remain calm and on the bit, with a relaxed jaw, slight arch to his neck, a lifted back and hind legs that step well forward under his belly.

- There should be an overtrack of one horseshoe's length beyond the front hoofprint.

- Medium walk is a good gait to use when introducing the horse to a new exercise such as lateral steps. It gives him time to establish the new work without being tiring and is often easier for the rider to learn how to co-ordinate his aiding.

## Collected walk

- In collected walk, the horse remains on the aids, showing energy but not speed. There will be a measure of self-carriage.

- He will be slightly taller and shorter in outline, with his head almost vertical. The poll is the highest point and the haunches a little lowered, as a result of greater flexing of all three hind limb joints.

- Collected walk should be the result of greater engagement of the hindquarters, so that they step well under the body, giving higher but rounder steps than in the medium.

- As a result of this increased engagement, the steps may be slightly shorter; the hind feet stepping into or very slightly behind, the front hoofprints. *Note that the aim of collection is for the hindquarters to carry more weight, and the by-product is a shorter, rounder step. Short steps are not the aim of collection.*

## Extended walk

- In the extension, the horse should cover the maximum ground that he is capable of, whilst maintaining the regularity of the steps. As a guide, the hind feet should touch the ground two shoes' length beyond the front hoofprints.

- The horse should not hurry.

- The outline will be a little longer, with more stretch to the head and neck, but the rider should still have contact with the bit.

*opposite, above* In this collected walk, Caroline's horse demonstrates activity and purpose, but without tension. The hind legs are engaged beneath the horse, enabling a shorter and taller outline. This would not happen if he was pulled short in the neck.

*opposite, below* Extended walk – note how the rider maintains a light contact and has allowed the horse to lengthen his position to encourage large, ground covering steps. Compare this to the free walk picture (page 27), where the horse is also covering maximum ground with his strides, but with loose reins.

# PROBLEMS WITH WALK

## 1. Breaks rhythm – pacing

A common cause is tension in the back.

### SOLUTIONS

**a** Using poles or low cavalletti can encourage freer steps and regularise the rhythm. An average distance between poles for walk work is 0.9m, but be prepared to alter this to suit the horse's stride length. See chapter 'Basic Training' for pole work suggestions.

**b** The rider needs to be able to feel what is going on in his horse, otherwise the timing of the aids is luck and this can affect the clarity of the gait.

  ◆ If the rider does have difficulty feeling the movement, then his trainer can ask him to call out the leg sequence to improve this.

  ◆ Riding without stirrups and with a deep seat will help the rider to feel the horse's motion and leg sequence clearly.

**c** Riding up and down hills is useful. If you ride positively downhill, it normally improves the walk to four clear beats.

**d** Ride transitions from free walk to medium and to free walk again. This will encourage relaxation of the horse's back muscles and the rider must take care to re-take the rein contact carefully, so as to keep the relaxed quality in the medium walk. Taking a strong hold will create tension that will affect the walk rhythm.

**e** Riding a walk shoulder-in is a good way to clear the pace to a correct four-beat rhythm.

**f** If the gait is very hurried, this can cause the walk to become lateral. We can try slowing the walk right down until the walk becomes four-beat again.

## 2. Walk is too fast/breaks into a jog

A nervous or excitable horse can display this problem. The solution must be to find ways of calming and relaxing him.

**a** We may need to be very patient and spend long periods in walk on a long rein to relax the horse.

*opposite page* Notice how the horse steps well under his body when walking uphill. This encourages bigger steps and loosens the back muscles. Downhill helps the horse find balance and have an awareness of his own body.

**b** The rider must sit very still and quietly, so that eventually the horse tunes into the rider's calm state and begins to relax too.

**c** Some horses become tense when they feel the rider's leg on their sides. Here we must keep our legs very light, so that he will gradually accept them without becoming tense. When this happens, we are in a position to improve the walk.

**d** Some young or cold-backed horses benefit from being lunged before ridden work. This gives them time to relax without the disturbance of the rider's weight on their back.

**e** We can use half-halts and frequent transitions to a square halt and walk again to gradually settle the walk.

## 3. Lazy walk

> *The walk should show regular, even steps with energy.*

The walk should show regular, even steps with energy. The horse should not drag his toe as he walks.

### SOLUTIONS

**a** We must ask for more activity.

- Try giving alternate leg aids, co-ordinated with each hind leg stepping forwards. We should feel the moment through our seat bones (see above). Apply the leg just before the hind foot on the same side leaves the ground.

**b** It is important that the rider is not tense or stiff in his back, or it will inhibit the horse's freedom to walk forwards freely.

**c** Strong rein contact can have the same effect. Try making small forward yields in the reins and keeping the wrists relaxed, to improve the quality of the walk, as the rider removes the 'handbrake'.

**d** Legs that constantly kick or grip tightly will dull the horse and make the walk feel lazy. The rider should keep a light touch with his legs on the horse's sides and use the aids sparingly, supported by a touch from the whip if necessary. When the horse responds, the rider must cease the aid and sit quietly with relaxed legs that 'drape' around the horse's sides. In time we can make him more sensitive to our aids.

**e** Riding over poles on the ground can improve the activity of the walk. Once the horse is negotiating them calmly, the distance between them can be *slightly* lengthened to encourage a longer stride. Pole work or low cavalletti can introduce some variety into the schooling and many horses enjoy this and we can therefore achieve improvements and give the horse some fun in his work.

An average horse distance for trotting poles is approximately 1.3m apart (less for ponies). Have an assistant on the ground to make any adjustments that are necessary.

**f** Making frequent transitions up and down will help bring the horse onto our aids more attentively.

# TROT

## General remarks

◆ The trot is a pace of two-time, the legs moving in regular diagonal pairs, with a clear moment of suspension between each pair touching the ground.

◆ The recognised varieties are working, medium, collected and extended.

## Working trot

◆ Working trot is the everyday trot, used with young or green horses that have yet to develop sufficient strength, suppleness and balance to show the other more advanced variants.

◆ The hind feet should 'track up' that is, step into the front hoofprints.

◆ The horse should show energy without running forward or leaning on the forehand.

◆ It is used when warming up and when stretching the horse for relaxation.

## Medium trot

◆ Here the steps show a medium amount of extension, that is midway between the horse's working and extended trot.

◆ The hind foot should over-track at least one shoe beyond the front hoofprint.

◆ The steps should remain rounded and not flatten or speed up. The horse stays on the bit, with a slightly longer outline and increased impulsion.

## Extended trot

- ◆ The extended trot shows the maximum reach of the horse's trot. His frame is slightly longer, but remains on the aids, with engaged haunches and a round and swinging back.

- ◆ As a guide, the hind feet will touch at least two horseshoes length beyond the front hoofprint.

- ◆ Owing to the increased physical demands, extensions are not expected at a novice level.

Expressive ground-covering steps in the extension, with the rider sitting perfectly still.

An incorrect extension because the horse is hollow. The under-neck muscle is braced showing that the horse is not on the aids. Some horses that are bred with huge movement can show bigger steps, but if it is not through and swinging, it is incorrect.

Here the rider is inhibiting the horse's movement by too much rein contact. It shortens the neck instead of allowing the horse to very slightly lengthen his outline.

This horse is out of balance and running on to his shoulders. This may happen if the rider asks for extension whilst the horse is not in balance; the extra power then pushes him onto his forehand.

## Collected trot

One can say that there are increasing levels of collection, meaning that when 'baby' collection is introduced through half-halts to balance the horse, it is not of the same degree as that shown by a Grand Prix trained horse.

◆ Collection requires the horse to be able to bend the joints of the hindquarters more markedly than in working trot, so that he is able to transfer weight from his forehand, and carry around 50 per cent or more on his haunches. This demands strength, suppleness and balance. It is not expected of a young horse, yet to develop physically and mentally under the added weight of a rider.

◆ In collected trot, the haunches will sink lower due to the greater flexing of the hind leg joints. Correspondingly, the forehand will seem to rise, creating an 'uphill' appearance which in turn leads to a lighter, more manoeuvrable horse, because he carries less weight on his forelegs.

Notice that the horse's head remains slightly in front of the vertical and that the neck is not pulled short to 'collect'.

◆ The outline will become a little shorter as the hind legs step closer to the forelegs, the back will be lifted and swinging, not tense, and the arch to the head and neck will be taller, with the poll the highest point.

◆ A rider who tries to collect only by shortening the neck will not experience this lighter forehand. It is a false collection.

◆ In collection, the steps will show marked cadence.

# PROBLEMS WITH TROT

## 1. Trot lacks suspension

When a horse is pushed too fast in the pursuit of impulsion, he becomes out of balance. This results in loss of suspension (see Glossary).

### SOLUTIONS

**a** Keep the trot active, but slow down the tempo. When the trot is too fast, the hind legs are often left out behind the horse. This means he is only able to propel himself forwards, rather than propel *and* carry weight, leading to flat steps.

◆ The fast trot will cause the horse to brace his head and neck to act as a counterbalance, giving the rider a heavy feel on the reins.

◆ Our aim is to achieve a better balance where the horse is able to show some airborne steps.

◆ When the horse's back is like an elastic swinging bridge, conveying un-interrupted energy from the haunches forward to the forehand, it is possible to have suspension in the trot.

**b** A flat trot can be seen in a horse that generally lacks suppleness. In this event we must work methodically to make him more athletic, to produce a happy athlete. This can easily take two or three months to show improvement. We can only proceed at the horse's rate; we should not try and force him as this will be mentally and physically harmful to him.

◆ Our programme will include many transitions, both between the gaits and within them. This especially helps with longitudinal suppleness.

◆ Lateral work will help improve suppleness. Leg-yield, shoulder-in and haunches-in are all appropriate exercises to teach our horse, as we work on his straightness. As he improves, half-passes and pirouettes can also be added.

Note: for descriptions of the aiding for these exercises, see the appropriate section of this book.

> *Our aim is to achieve a better balance where the horse is able to show some airborne steps.*

> *We can only proceed at the horse's rate; we should not try and force him as this will be mentally and physically harmful to him.*

c Conformation can be a factor. Short-backed horses with low-set necks or heavy forehand may lack lift in the trot. They require tact and patience in their training as their bodies are not the ideal build. However, an experienced trainer can often achieve good results, although it may take longer than with a horse that is blessed with good conformation.

- The rider must have the horse on his seat aids, so that if the horse becomes heavy on his forehand, he is not tempted to hold him up with his hands, which worsens the problem. Instead he needs to be able to control the horse's speed with his seat, thus freeing up the hands from being the brakes.

- When the horse is listening to the seat aids, the rider can gradually use a combination of leg and seat aids to channel the energy into balanced steps that show some spring.

## 2. Head up in transition

Causes can include the horse not accepting the contact, or a lack of throughness and engagement.

a Is the contact too strong? Harsh hands hurt the horse's mouth and cause him to brace his jaw in defence, leading to him throwing his head up in a transition.

*Keep the wrists supple and giving at all times and think 'forwards' with the contact.*

- The answer is to ride with a softer, more allowing feel in the reins. During half-halts the hands must remain in place over the withers and not pull backwards. Keep the wrists supple and giving at all times and think 'forwards' with the contact.

- An unbalanced rider may jerk the reins and cause the head up. The trainer must help the rider to improve his seat so that he does not need the reins for support. This could involve exercises on the lunge, such as work without stirrups, stretching exercises for suppleness and working without holding the reins.

b A stiff, unbalanced horse that is on the forehand and lacks throughness, often throws his head up in a transition. As the cause is a lack of connection from hock to bridle, the solution lies in gymnastic work to loosen his body.

- A stiff horse cannot easily engage the hind legs under the body to 'lift' himself into a transition, rather, he braces his neck to 'lever' himself into it.

- The rider needs to work on the longitudinal suppleness, which means many transitions between and within the paces.

♦ Working the horse in a stretched position, with the poll at wither-height to encourage him to seek the bit with a lower neck, will help achieve a lifting back. How long this takes depends on the individual horse. The idea is to achieve a silhouette in which the horse's back is like the top of a wheel, slightly convex, not concave. When done correctly, he will move with the under-neck muscle soft and a visible 'up and down' swing behind the saddle.

♦ We can work him in trot over small cavalletti to relax his whole body and most horses enjoy this work.

♦ Once the horse is relaxed and swinging, we can begin to put him together, connecting hocks to bridle with quiet forward pushing aids, to engage the hind legs under his body.

♦ It would be very wrong to try and fix his head into position with gadgets or a strong bit, as neither deal with the source of the problem and would result in discomfort for the horse and leave him moving stiffly.

♦ For further thoughts, see 'Going Above the Bit' in the next chapter.

## 3. Difficulty in producing medium trot

♦ There is little or no response to the aids from the horse

♦ The horse responds by running faster.

### WHY DOES THIS MATTER?

♦ A basic training goal is to develop the range of the horse's natural gaits.

♦ One measure of a horse's suppleness is how adjustable he is within the gaits.

♦ Transitions within the gaits are an integral part of training the dressage horse and, as they appear at almost every level of competition, the rider must have strategies to develop the differences in the gaits, especially in those horses that are not born with extravagant paces.

### SOLUTIONS

a The first question should be, 'Did I ask correctly?' If the horse does not understand your aids because they were unclear, then he cannot be blamed for not responding.

♦ This would be like you asking somebody to do something in a foreign language, but using the wrong words. They may guess what you mean, or they may do nothing because they cannot understand you. Repeating the same mistake will not help them to understand what you want!

◆ A rider who has made a mistake should not punish the horse for his own shortcomings, but should check that he has prepared the horse with half-halts. These warn him that you are about to ask for something different and also physically prepare the horse by momentarily steadying the speed and engaging the hind legs under his torso to improve his balance prior to asking for the medium steps.

◆ This makes it easier for the horse to make the transition: because the leg aid has called up more power, balance and throughness have been confirmed, so the impulsion can be channelled positively.

◆ Having prepared the transition, the rider's upper body remains tall and poised, the inside leg then closes at the girth in rhythm with the steps to ask for longer strides. The hands should be still and relaxed to maintain the same contact, as if presenting an open door for the horse to step through. It is normal to allow the horse to lengthen his position very slightly to allow the medium steps.

◆ The medium trot should appear bold without rushing. Imagine the medium steps as like a 'stretched' collected trot; the horse remaining round, balanced and with marked suspension in the steps, but with greater ground-covering strides and an 'uphill' appearance.

**b** If the rider aids correctly, but there is still little or no response, then we need to review the horse's basic reactions to our aids. (See Chapter 4, page 55)

**c** Where the horse runs faster instead of showing the medium steps, we must consider the reason.

◆ With a young or under-developed horse, weakness in the haunches can be the cause.

◆ The hindquarters need to be stronger to maintain medium steps than in the working trot. This is because he has to support more of his own body-weight when the hind leg engages further under his torso to give the medium trot.

◆ Pay attention to improving his body strength. Cavalletti work, hacking in the country, as well as time in the arena are all part of our programme. Shoulder-in, haunches-in and transitions will all contribute to building strength.

**d** Conformation can have an influence. A horse that is croup-high can find it difficult if he is built 'downhill'.

- A young horse may even out and no longer be croup-high when he finishes growing. Until this time, it would be sensible to moderate requests for medium trot. If a horse is incapable of performing the task then we risk teaching him the wrong way of going and possibly create tension in our horse.

- We should spend time building the strength and improving the balance of our young horse, without overtaxing his body (see above).

- With a mature horse that is croup-high, we must realise that there may be limitations on what he can achieve. Nonetheless, our training will try to improve the horse's ability to lower the haunches and carry more weight to improve his balance. Our programme must be carefully monitored so that we do not push him too hard; the horse must be our calendar so that we progress at a pace comfortable for his physique.

**e** If a crooked horse is asked for medium trot, it will not be successful. He is not in balance, so asking for a medium trot will make this worse, leading to running steps.

- A crooked horse does not work evenly with his hind legs. Asking for medium trot will exaggerate this, leading to uneven steps.

- Using counter-canter can help straightness and the canter energy can also lend power to the trot, helping to produce very good medium trot steps.

# CANTER

## General remarks

- Canter is a pace of three beats.

- It is referred to as 'right' or 'left' canter depending on which is the leading leg.

- The leg sequence is:
  1. Outside hind leg.
  2. Inside hind leg and outside foreleg *together* as a pair.
  3. Inside foreleg.

- After beat 3, (the 'leading' leg) there is a moment of suspension, when there are no hooves touching the ground.

◆ On average a working canter stride covers approximately one horse's length (roughly 3m for a horse, less for a pony).

◆ For competition we recognise working, medium, collected and extended canter. Working canter is the everyday variant.

◆ With a young horse it is normal to develop the medium canter before collection. This is to ensure that the horse has energy and that collection does not result in merely a short, lifeless stride.

## Canter aids

◆ The rider sits with inside positioning (see page 54) and prepares the horse mentally and physically with soft half-halts. This warns him that you are about to ask for something different and improves his balance and engagement.

◆ With the inside shoulder slightly back and stepping down into the inside stirrup iron, more weight is placed on the inside seat bone.

◆ The inside rein shows slight flexion to the inside, enough to see the horse's inside eye, but no more. Maintain a light contact.

This medium canter shows clear lift in the strides, besides positive forward energy.

In collection there should be as much energy as in the medium canter but it is expressed in a different form. The haunches carry more weight and the impulsion produces taller, rounder strides.

This photograph shows that in extended canter, the horse 'sits' down behind the saddle, producing big, 'uphill' strides.

- The outside rein supports and controls the outside shoulder, but without pulling.

- Keep the inside leg passive at the girth and use it after the canter transition to ask for good energy and 'jump' in the strides.

- The outside leg is about one or two hand widths behind the girth and with a light touch signals to the horse to make the canter departure. This is best given when the outside foreleg is on the ground. This should guarantee the correct strike off.

- Once cantering, the rider's outside leg becomes passive, unless correcting drifting to the outside. If it is clamped onto the horse's side, it may unintentionally cause him to carry his haunches to the inside.

# PROBLEMS WITH CANTER

## 1. Crookedness

For advice on dealing with a crooked canter, see page 63.

## 2. Wrong strike-off

This happens when the horse does not canter on the lead asked for by the rider. A common cause is poor preparation before the transition.

### SOLUTIONS

a  Check your weight aid. If your seat slips to the outside as you ask for canter, this can unbalance the horse and cause the wrong strike-off.

   To apply the weight aid, be sure to sit with 'inside positioning' so that your inside shoulder is brought a little back, along with the outside leg behind the girth, which places slightly more weight on the inside seat bone. It can help if you think of stepping down into the inside stirrup too.

b  Be sure the leg position is correct, with the outside leg one to two hand widths behind the girth. This is the leg which starts the canter. If it slips forward, then it is very difficult for the horse to understand which is the outside and which is the inside leg, causing confusion and possibly a wrong strike-off.

   - Do not take the outside leg any further back than this; it may irritate the horse, leading to bucking or kicking out.

◆ The inside leg should prepare the horse for the transition by activating the haunches and maintaining the inside bend, but it should be passive at the moment of transition. Therefore, with only the outside leg asking for the canter, we try to make it clear to the horse which lead we require.

c Allowing the trot to 'run' prior to the transition will make it difficult for the horse.

◆ Keep the tempo unhurried yet active, so that he is in balance longitudinally from tail to poll.

## SUGGESTED EXERCISES

◆ It can help an inexperienced rider to count the beats of the trot preceding the canter transition, 'one-two, one-two' and so on. The speed of counting should remain constant as the moment of transition approaches.

◆ Using a direct transition from walk to canter will be helpful. The horse will not be able to use momentum to dive into canter on his forehand, but it will encourage him to bend his hocks and lift himself into canter correctly.

◆ In trot, ride 10m circles until the horse is steady and balanced. Then ask quietly for the canter. Correctly ridden small circles are a good way to steady a rushing horse. See photos overleaf.

◆ Ride shoulder-in, then straighten and immediately ask for the canter transition. The lateral work should improve the horse's balance and engage the inside hind leg, so that your horse can lift himself calmly into canter.

*Correctly ridden small circles are a good way to steady a rushing horse.*

d If the horse is very stiff on one rein, he may favour cantering on the other lead. Here the rider needs to think about softening the bend to the inside to achieve a straighter, more supple horse.

## SUGGESTED EXERCISE

◆ On the stiff rein, spiral a 20m circle down to as small as the horse can manage without losing his rhythm and balance – perhaps 8 or 10m diameter. Then spiral out to a large circle, pushing the horse out with the inside leg at the girth to ask him to bend his ribcage a little around the inside aid. Try to think that your inside leg is pushing the horse *off* the inside rein and *up* to the outside rein, so that the horse, not the rider, contacts the bit. Making small forward yields with the inside (stiff) rein during the spiralling can help to wean the horse away from using the inside rein as a crutch to lean on for his balance.

The rider ensures a uniform bend from poll to tail that matches the pattern on the ground. This produces an aligned horse that can find a better balance. The sequence moves from right to left.

- Remember to keep the outside leg in position behind the girth to prevent the horse evading the bending by pushing his haunches out. When you reach the large circle, ask for the inside canter lead.

- Alternatively, if you feel that your horse is in good balance and rhythm when on the small circle, then you can ask for the transition there and spiral out in canter. It is wise to canter only large circles until the horse is feeling more supple and balanced in both directions.

**e** If the rider is too strong in the outside rein contact, this can cause the wrong lead. Make subtle yields before the transition so that the contact is like an elastic band. When the horse is more relaxed in the rein contact and able to show a soft bend to the inside, then ask for the strike-off.

- The trainer may ask the rider to show some give and re-taking of the reins, with one, then both, reins to encourage the rider to become aware of how strong his hands are. The horse should remain in the same speed and rhythm when the rein is given. However if the horse throws his head up during the give and re-take, then the hands are too strong.

- One of the functions of the outside rein is to control the amount of inside neck positioning; but this does not mean that it should be used like a vice! If we are

too strong in our outside rein, we cause discomfort and tension in our horse. Our aim should be to have control with the minimum, not maximum aiding.

**f** Because of stiffness, some horses evade the inside bend by pushing the haunches out at the moment of transition.

## SUGGESTED EXERCISES

◆ Use travers on a circle to school the haunches-inwards a little. *The angle only needs to be enough to create the correct alignment in the horse's spine and forehand.*

◆ The rider should also take care to keep his weight slightly to the inside and that the horse is not able to push him to the outside of the saddle.

◆ Riding a large walk pirouette, then cantering, is also a useful exercise. The rider must be sensitive to his horse and only ask for a few pirouette steps and not too small, otherwise it will be impossible for the horse to offer what we want.

◆ If a crooked horse is allowed to fall onto his outside shoulder in the transition he may offer the wrong lead.

◆ To correct this, reduce the inside neck bend; the outside rein should only allow sufficient neck positioning for the rider to see the inside eye of the horse.

- Riding shoulder-fore prior to the transition can be helpful if the horse is very one sided and does not easily accept the outside rein's controlling action.

- Riding leg-yield from the outside track inwards to the three-quarter line and then asking for the inside lead can help. The idea is that we use the leg-yield in this way to straighten the horse prior to the transition.

Imagine the horse is crooked to the right and bends his body, leaning too much weight onto the left shoulder. To correct this, try leg-yielding inwards from the track to the three-quater line. As you approach the corner, ask for a small bend to the inside, and then aid for right-lead canter in the corner.

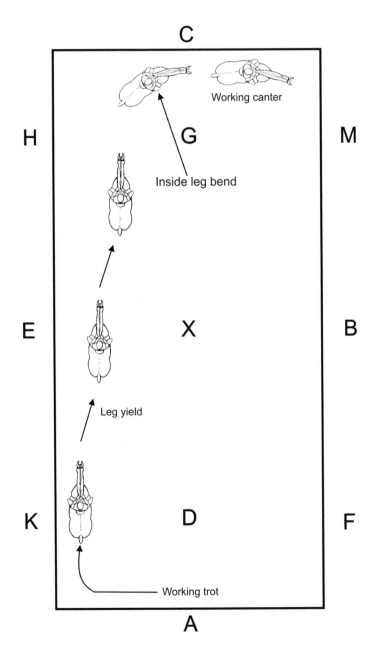

C

Working canter

H    G    M

Inside leg bend

E    X    B

Leg yield

K    D    F

Working trot

A

◆ A more advanced exercise would be to ride renvers on the long side of the arena, (the horse would be bent around our left leg in this example) then straighten the horse and make the canter transition. The renvers is an excellent suppling exercise, as in this instance it asks the horse to bend his body away from his hollow side. When we finish the lateral steps, we should be able to place the horse with the correct alignment before the transition.

> **Remember the principle** If your horse does not bend enough (is stiff) then bend his body more – but if he bends too much (crooked or hollow) then bend him less. The aim is to have a straight (aligned) horse at all times.

## 3. Runs into canter

When the canter transition is made, the speed should stay the same.

### SOLUTIONS

a The first consideration is whether the rider has prepared the transition by making correct half-halts. This should become automatic for every transition. If it is omitted then the rider is not giving the horse a chance to make a good transition.

> **Half-halts** We can say there are three parts to a half-halt; seat, leg and rein aids.
>
> 1. The rider applies the seat aid by growing taller in the saddle and firming up the muscles in the abdomen and lower back areas. This is so that the horse feels a resistance from the rider's pelvis and it will prevent the hind legs from quickening when the horse feels the next element, the leg aids.
>
> 2. The rider closes his legs on the horse to push the hind legs further underneath the horse's body to increase engagement and balance.
>
> 3. The rider gives a rein aid, by making a vibration along the outside rein. Some people describe this action as like squeezing water out of a sponge. It asks the horse to soften his lower jaw and in co-ordination with the seat and leg aids, steadies the horse making him ready for a transition (between or within the paces), turn, or to collect him. ➡

4. This rein vibration is brief and the moment the rider feels the horse make a slight response, he must yield the rein more softly to reward the horse and to tell him he has done the right thing. This softening must not be forgotten! Note that this yield is not as in a give and re-take of the reins where the rein is made slack, but is an allowing rein, to reduce the contact.

5. Riders must take care that the hand delivers the rein aid at the withers and does not pull backwards. To do so will cause the horse to stiffen his jaw and poll, the opposite of what we wish.

b If the horse is fresh or anticipating a canter transition, he may hurry into it. The rider can try riding a series of 10m circles in different parts of the arena to steady the horse and improve his balance. When he listens to the aids more attentively, then the rider can make a quiet half-halt and then tactfully ask for the canter.

◆ If the horse is not listening to the steadying aids, we can ask for rein-back, and then proceed quietly before asking for the canter. This may need repeating a few times if the horse is excited or very strong in the contact.

◆ It can be that the horse is quite sharp in his reactions to the leg, causing him to rush the transition. Here the rider must carefully prepare the horse as usual, but give the lightest of outside leg aids. Sometimes it can be enough to have the seat and legs in the correct positions but barely touching the horse's sides and think 'canter' and it will happen. (As you are thinking canter, a sensitive horse will notice a slight forward indication from your inside seat bone and this can be enough.)

◆ If the rider notices that the horse is anticipating the transition and speeding up, then vary the place in the arena where the canter is asked for.

◆ To keep the horse obedient, make a downward transition just before the place where the horse is anticipating canter; or make a circle or change rein. The rider must keep the initiative in the schooling session!

c A long or weak-backed horse may have difficulty in making a clean transition. He may substitute speed for balance and engagement to make the transition.

◆ The long-term solution is to devise a gymnastic programme for your horse to strengthen his weak areas, which may include jumping grids of low cavalletti and hacking in the countryside besides arena work.

- Sitting too strongly can lead to a weak horse hollowing his back down like a hammock, making a correct transition impossible.

- In the short term, the weak horse can benefit if the rider adopts a light seat; naturally he must be in balance and not reliant on the reins for stability.

- The upper body is inclined slightly forward to reduce the weight in the saddle, although the seat does not leave the saddle. More weight is taken by the knees and thighs. It can be helpful to ride with the stirrup leathers a hole or two shorter for light seat work.

**d** Another cause of running into canter can be a rider who is too strong in his hands. This will create a stiff, pulling horse who tries to run away from the harsh feeling in his mouth.

- The solution is to remember the basics; use the seat, legs and reins together, with half-halts that soften as soon as they feel a positive response from the horse. The horse needs to be on ('under the control of') the rider's seat, so that he is not using the reins like a handbrake in a car. When the rider can make a give and re-take of both reins without the horse speeding up or losing balance or outline, then there is a measure of self-carriage and a canter transition can be ridden without quickening.

## 4. The canter is four beat

A four-beat canter happens when, instead of moving as a pair, the inside hind touches the ground before the outside foreleg, producing four beats instead of three.

### WHY DOES THIS MATTER?

A natural canter has three beats per stride. It is a fundamental principle of dressage that we train to preserve and enhance, not break down, the horse's natural gaits.

### SOLUTIONS

**a** A common cause of this problem is trying to obtain collection incorrectly.

- Collection is about how much weight the horse can carry on his hind legs, *not* how short we can make his stride.

- When a rider forgets his leg and seat aids and uses the reins too much to shorten the strides, it can stifle the impulsion and stiffen the horse's back, leading to a four-beat canter.

- The answer is to focus less on the hands, but use seat, legs and reins harmoniously, so the horse can work through his back and better engage the hind legs.

- To achieve this, the rider may need to make some give and re-takes of the reins, to encourage self-carriage and to lighten his contact to give the horse the confidence of seeking and then accepting the contact.

> *If there is no energy, there is nothing to collect.*

- The inside leg has to ask for the stride to 'jump' with energy. If there is no energy, there is nothing to collect.

b  It can be that the canter is too slow with insufficient impulsion; the answer is to increase the activity of the hind legs whilst containing the speed with the seat.

- Sometimes simply riding the canter more forward for a long side or two of the arena can freshen up the energy levels and clear the faulty four-beat canter.

c  A horse who is very stiff in his back and hocks can show a four-beat canter, especially when the rider tries to slow the speed. Such a horse may pull himself along rapidly with his forelegs, so that when the rider attempts to slow down, the horse breaks to a four-beat canter.

- First establish whether there is a medical reason why the horse finds the canter so difficult and if there is a lameness issue. If not, then the rider needs to embark on a programme to improve suppleness.

> *We should also not forget to check that the saddle is a comfortable fit for our horse.*

- Using cavalletti in a grid and poles on the ground to trot over can be very helpful, along with many transitions both between and within the gaits, which are very good at improving the longitudinal suppleness.

- Lateral work would also be very useful both to improve suppleness and to help the horse step further under his body with the hocks, thus learning to accept more weight on them.

- We should also not forget to check that the saddle is a comfortable fit for our horse; otherwise it can cause discomfort and lead to problems in the gaits.

## 5. Disunited canter (cross-cantering)

A disunited canter is where the forelegs follow the pattern of one lead and the hind legs follow the pattern of the other lead. This is characterised by a very 'bumpy' feeling for the rider, rather than the normal, smooth 'rocking horse' sensation.

## SOLUTIONS

**a** An unbalanced or weak horse can often become disunited, especially If he is asked to canter a small circle.

- In the short term, the rider should moderate his demands and ride easier patterns with his horse.

- Avoid working the horse in a small space; he will appreciate the extra room until his strength and balance improve.

- The arena surface is also important. If it is uneven or loose, the horse can lose confidence in the footing and this can lead him to become disunited.

**b** An unbalanced rider can be the cause. A sensitive or weak horse can easily become disunited if the rider cannot sit quietly in the saddle.

- When in right-lead canter, be sure to sit with your body in 'position right' (and vice versa for left lead). See overleaf for description.

- Take care to sit still in the saddle. The rider's head and shoulders should not rock during canter, only the hips. Also, the shoulders should remain parallel to the horse's shoulders and not twist from side to side. Either can be enough to cause the disunited canter.

- If the rider is dependent of the reins for balance, this can cause the disunited canter.

The trainer needs to work with the rider to improve his seat. Lunge lessons can be most helpful. When the rider is able to show the confidence and depth of seat to be able to ride with relaxed, supple wrists and hands that demonstrate a forward thinking contact, then the disunited problem can disappear.

- The rider should not forget that we often achieve a more round and relaxed outline by giving the rein forwards slightly to make a contact rather than keeping a tight, backwards hold of the horse's mouth.

**c** A disunited canter is sometimes seen when counter-canter is introduced, especially if the rider is attempting too much too quickly. A stiff, unbalanced horse may easily become disunited during counter-canter.

- The rider must sit and maintain inside positioning during counter-canter – and note that this means to the inside of the *horse's* bend, not to the *centre* of the arena.

◆ The rider's weight aid can make a big difference to the horse's balance, so it is very important to sit with inside positioning at all times, so that your weight remains more into the inside seat bone. If the upper body shifts to the outside, the weight will change to the wrong side and this can make the canter disunited.

◆ If the horse becomes disunited as you attempt to ride counter-canter around a corner, make the turn larger. Shallow corners are easier for the horse, but if this is still too difficult, correct back a stage and try riding single serpentine loops to re-establish his balance and confidence. This is an example of 'taking time, but not wasting it'!

◆ For further thoughts on riding counter-canter, please see the Counter-Canter section on page 144.

## Position right or left

The rider adopts position right of left whenever he bends the horse for turns, circles, lateral work and when in canter. It means we sit with the inside shoulder a little back, parallel to the horse's shoulders, to place more weight on our inside seat bone. The inside leg is at the girth, the outside leg behind the girth. The rider looks forwards between the horse's ears.

# 4

# BASIC TRAINING PROBLEMS

## 1. The horse does not react to the leg ('not in front of the leg')

This is when the horse is slow or reluctant to respond promptly to the rider's leg aid.

### WHY DOES IT MATTER?

We need to train our horse to react promptly to our aids; otherwise the quality of the work and rider's ability to make corrections will be affected.

> The ideal we aim for is for the horse to be 'on the aids' or 'in front of the leg', which implies that he is fully focused on his rider and responds promptly and appropriately to the rider's light leg aids.

### SOLUTIONS

a There can be a number of causes for this problem. The horse may not understand what is being asked of him, therefore is hesitant and lacks confidence, making him slow to react. Consider whether the aids are being applied correctly and with good timing.

◆ For example, if the rider's lower leg swings around, the horse will feel it accidentally bumping his sides in different places. He thinks this is an aid, responds forwards, but the rider pulls on the reins, not realising he was the cause of it. This confuses the horse so that in future he does not know whether to respond to the leg in case it leads to another pull on his mouth.

♦ In this example the solution clearly lies with the rider and he must work on his seat position in the saddle to improve the stability of his lower leg. This could include work on the lunge without stirrups and ensuring that the lower back is supple so that a deep seat can be maintained at all paces.

b Strong hands can be the root of the problem. Again the rider needs help with his seat, trying to improve his balance so that he does not use the reins to keep himself in the saddle. Only a rider who can remain in balance independent of the reins and stirrups for support can achieve good hands.

c Behind the leg can be a tack issue – 'is the bit too strong for my horse?'

♦ The horse may have a sensitive mouth and be afraid of going forward if the bit is severe and the rider's hands are not subtle. An experienced trainer can advise whether a milder bit would be more suitable and encourage the horse to relax and go more freely forward from the leg aids. Our aim should be that our horses go happily in a simple snaffle bit with a cavesson noseband, or a correctly fitted drop or flash noseband if he opens his mouth.

♦ Later the double bridle can be introduced, but only when the horse is accepting the snaffle correctly and the rider has achieved a level of sophistication in his riding skills. The double or full bridle should never be used as strong brakes, or to manipulate the head and neck carriage into an arched position.

♦ When our horse has been trained to a level where all the work can be achieved harmoniously in the snaffle bridle, then the double can be used to add refinement to the aids.

d A lazy or phlegmatic horse may be slow to react to our leg aids. We can sensitise him to our legs by making many transitions, both between the gaits and within them. By doing this we focus the horse's mind, and the frequency of the transitions will bring him onto our aids and can also make the hind legs active.

♦ If he is dull to our leg aids, kicking his sides is likely to cause resentment and further deaden his responses. Keep the legs light and, if he ignores the aid, tap him with the schooling whip by your inside leg.

♦ It is important to time this with the leg aid so that the horse associates leg and whip as meaning the same thing. This way we can teach the horse to respond to light touches from the legs.

e If the horse is feeling sluggish, then we can raise his adrenalin levels with some canter work. After warming up, try some canter in a light seat. Encourage him to make some tempo changes, whilst maintaining control and balance. The

> Aiding is a system of communication based on 'negative reinforcement'.
>
> A horse has to understand what our system of touches and pressures on his body mean. An aid is a stimulus to prompt a response from our horse.
>
> For example, when we wish him to trot, we touch him with our inside leg. As soon as he does so, we cease the leg pressure. Then our horse will learn that he 'earns' a quiet leg from his rider by reacting promptly.
>
> When the horse is doing what we wish, we show approval by sitting still and harmonising with his movement.
>
> We can see that the rider must have control of his own body if he is to be able to educate a horse in dressage.

priority is to activate our horse, as it is his *energy* we channel when we put him on the bit, and without controlled energy we have nothing.

**f** Some horses can become stale and lethargic if their routine never varies. For them we can vary the day to day work programme.

- Include some hacking in the country once or twice a week.

- Use some small cavalletti. This can be fun for the horse and sharpen his responses to our aids. It is also a good way to gymnasticise the horse, so that we achieve one of our aims in a different way to normal.

- Take your horse to different arenas occasionally. A different environment may make the dull horse brighter and easier to ride.

- Some horses thrive when they are worked in company and this may help improve his responses to the aids.

**g** If the horse is young or physically weak, fatigue can slow his reactions to our legs. Consider changing the work programme to shorter sessions so that you can finish whilst he is still fresh and enjoying his work. If possible, ride twice a day but for shorter periods so that he can recover his energy in between. Continuing to work a tired horse is a mistake and can lead to evasions and napping.

- We can also review the horse's diet, to ensure he is fed a balanced regime that provides all the carbohydrates, proteins, fats, vitamins and minerals he needs to perform his work.

- If you are not sure, then seek the advice of an equine nutritionist.

## 2. The horse goes above the bit

### WHAT IS IT?

A horse is said to be above the bit when he carries his head too high and in such a way that the bit no longer operates correctly on the bars of the mouth.

### WHY IS IT IMPORTANT?

A horse that is above the bit is likely to be, tense, stiff and hollow in his back. His hind legs will not be engaged under his body, therefore he will not be in balance. All of these problems are encompassed when we describe a horse as working above the bit.

It is a mistake to focus only on the head and neck position.

A correctly arched neck, with the horse carrying his head slightly in front of the vertical and jaw relaxed, should be the result of the whole horse being supple, balanced, with engaged hind legs, and mentally tuned to the rider. This is a horse that is 'on the aids'.

As training progresses, we aim to develop his strength so that he can work towards self carriage, in other words, not relying on the rider's hands for supporting his balance.

> *It is a mistake to focus only on the head and neck position.*

### SOLUTIONS

a Harsh hands can cause a horse to be above the bit. A trainer must assess whether this is due to poor rider balance, leading to balancing on the reins, or a misunderstanding of the correct application of the aids.

- ◆ In the first case the trainer may suggest working without stirrups to deepen the seat, or lunge lessons to improve the rider's balance and develop an independent seat.

- ◆ Working without reins whilst on the lunge can help to break the habit of resorting to pulling the reins to stabilise position.

- ◆ A good lunge exercise is to hold the pommel with the outside hand, whilst allowing the inside arm to hang loose by the side. This helps the rider to find his balance and, when feeling secure, the trainer can encourage him to let go of the pommel and to focus on finding the horse's rhythm through a supple back and swinging pelvis.

When a rider over-uses his hands to control the horse rather than co-ordinating leg, seat and rein aids, the horse is likely to go above the bit to avoid the

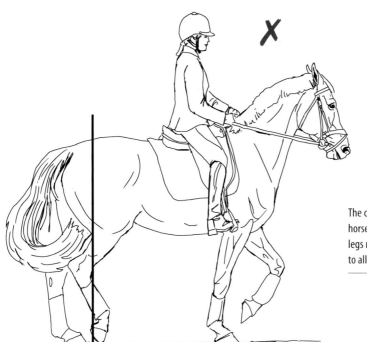

The contact is too strong, so the horse's head is high, with the hind legs not far enough under his body to allow him to work on the bit.

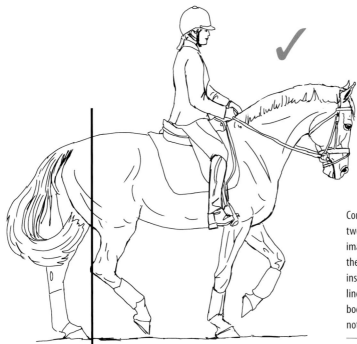

Compare the inside hock position in these two diagrams; as a guide to engagement, imagine a perpendicular line drawn from the outside stifle to the ground. When the inside hock is able to flex in front of this line, the horse is stepping well under his body. When it flexes behind this line, he is not engaging.

discomfort in his mouth. Here the trainer needs to take time to explain fully what is required.

- It is the trainer's job to educate the rider to use his aids sympathetically for the well-being of the horse and because the results gained in this way produce a more natural and elegant way of going, which are the fundamentals of Classical training.

*It is the trainer's job to educate the rider to use his aids sympathetically for the well-being of the horse...*

**b** A young horse with a weak back needs time to become accustomed to the rider's weight before he is able to work with a rounder topline. However, if the rider pulls or forces the head and neck down, producing a false outline, it can lead to a stiff back and strained joints in the inexperienced horse.

**c** Conformation can be a factor.

- A long-backed horse is often weaker and needs time to develop the strength needed to carry his rider's weight. Whilst this strengthening work is being carried out, the horse should be allowed a slightly longer position so that we do not force him into a false outline.

- A horse who has a short, deep neck and is thick through the gullet may initially find it uncomfortable to work in the correct position. He should be ridden a little more 'open' in his head and neck position until the muscles are accustomed to the work. With both of these examples we are reminded of the principle that we should 'take time, but not waste it' in training.

**d** An out-of-balance horse will frequently work above the bit.

- If the rider drives him too fast, the horse is pushed onto his forehand, with the hind legs trailing. This leads to the horse bracing his neck and raising his head upwards.

- Correct this by slowing the tempo and make soft half-halts to encourage a softer jaw and poll. Then it becomes possible for him to relax and step under his body with the hocks.

- Naturally the degree of engagement will depend on the horse's age and level of training, but the building blocks of correct training are founded in the horse working on the bit, not above it.

**e** Conversely, if a horse works with insufficient energy from the hindquarters, this also causes him to go above the bit. When the paces lack energy, the hocks trail behind the horse, leaving him on the forehand as he uses his head and neck as a balancing pole.

- The solution is to energise the gait, but take care not to confuse speed with impulsion; otherwise the horse will be driven onto his shoulders.

- If the horse is lazy, it can help to do some canter work, or frequent transitions to raise his adrenalin levels and, when he is more responsive, the rider can return to the task of putting the horse correctly on the aids. This is an example of recognising the correct priority in training; that we cannot work the horse on the aids until he makes prompt responses to the rider's requests.

f A crooked horse cannot be said to correctly work on the bit, as the hind legs are not working evenly and the rein contact will be compromised. See point 4 for suggestions on dealing with crookedness.

g We should not forget that ill-fitting tack or even insects can cause enough discomfort so that the horse will not settle to his work and goes above the bit.

- Physical pain or discomfort will distract the horse from working on the bit.

- Some horses are very sensitive to flies biting them and cannot focus on the rider's aids when they are bothered in this way. Consider using an ear bonnet to protect the ears and a fly repellent to ward off the insects.

## 3. Going behind the bit

This is when the horse carries his nose behind the perpendicular and possibly tries to drop the bit altogether.

### WHY DOES THIS MATTER?

This is an evasion of the contact and thus affects everything we try to do in training.

### SOLUTIONS

a Strong or rough hands are often the cause. The horse attempts to avoid the pressure on the bars of his mouth by drawing his head back towards his chest, so that we see an over-shortening of the neck.

- The rider must work patiently to build the horse's confidence by keeping his hands and wrists soft and flexible whilst maintaining closed hands. At the same time the rider needs to take care to use his leg aids to push the horse up to the bit to establish a genuine contact.

As a general rule, if the horse works too short in his neck, we need to ride him a little more open in order to attain the correct outline of nose on or just in front of the vertical, with engaged hocks and swinging back.

If the opposite is true, and the horse is too long, we need to close him from the *haunches forward towards the bit*, so that we create longitudinal flexion and an outline appropriate for his level of training.

Note that this does not mean pulling the reins; this causes a stiff, uncomfortable horse that does not move through his body.

**b** Asking for too much collection before the horse is sufficiently engaged can lead to this problem.

- If this is the case, the rider should take more time and allow the horse to work in an appropriate outline, rather than forcing the neck too short. It is a tenet of training that the outline is created by the level of strength and engagement of the haunches, not the other way around.

**c** Nervous or excitable horses can have an irregular contact; sometimes above the bit and sometimes behind it. Here the rider needs to be sensitive to his horse and proceed tactfully and quietly with light hands. Should the horse jump forward unexpectedly it is important that the rider does not grab at the reins, which will make the problem worse and confirm to the horse that there is something to worry about.

**d** Going behind the bit can be caused because the bit is too severe. The obvious course is to select a milder bit so that the horse can regain his confidence and step forward to the rein contact.

It can be that the rider swaps the normal bit for a stronger alternative because he feels the horse is leaning and he wants to have him 'lighter in his hand'. Although this is a valid wish, it is approaching the problem the wrong way. A lighter contact comes from having the horse balanced, engaged and supple through his back. Then, when his hind legs step well under his body, it enables weight to be transferred from forehand to haunches so that we feel a lightening of the forehand. When we can do this, we are dealing with the cause of the problem, not merely tinkering with the symptoms.

# 4. Crookedness

Crookedness is when the hind legs do not follow the path of the forelegs. We may see too much head and neck bend and the haunches may be carried to one side. The horse is 'out of alignment'.

## WHY DOES IT MATTER?

◆ Dealing with crookedness and developing a 'straight' horse is *absolutely fundamental in training*.

◆ A straight horse will have equal muscle development on each side of his body and therefore be able to perform the work equally on both reins. A crooked horse has uneven muscle development; imagine a human weightlifter with one strong side and one weak side and you will see that it simply would not work!

◆ As a crooked horse does not work equally with both hind legs, he is unable to collect. It will also compromise his ability to show medium or extended paces as he will lose rhythm, suspension and regularity.

◆ Like humans, horses are left- or right-sided, and our goal must be to develop an ambidextrous athlete.

◆ Crookedness will not get better by itself. The rider must have a programme of gymnastic exercises that will address any unevenness in the horse.

◆ When working on a single track, the aim is for the hind hooves to follow exactly the corresponding front hooves and for the hind legs to work equally. Thus, when the horse's back lifts and swings, the rider feels an even contact in each rein.

◆ If riding a turn or circle, then there should be a uniform curve along the spine that runs from the root of the tail to the poll. This will give us a 'straight' or aligned horse, which is vital for the even gymnastic development of our horse.

If the rider drops the inside shoulder and collapses the inside hip, this will push his weight to the outside and unbalance the horse enough to cause the canter to become crooked.

## SOLUTIONS: THE RIDER

◆ We should assess the rider's seat before we blame the horse! A crooked rider in the saddle will make a crooked horse.

◆ See chapter on 'The Seat' for further advice.

## To straighten the crooked horse

We cannot straighten a crooked horse by pulling on the stiff rein. The cause of crookedness is often associated with one hind leg (on the soft or hollow side) avoiding taking weight due to lack of strength. So we must encourage that leg to work a little harder so that the horse is persuaded to step up to the bit and contact it on the soft or hollow side. If we can do this, coupled with soft half-halts to ask the horse to relax his jaw on the stiff or strong side, straightness can be achieved.

## Falling-in

Falling-in is when the horse cuts inside the line of a turn or circle rather than his body and hooves following the curvature of the line. It is the mirror image of falling out and both indicate that the horse is not 'straight'.

Falling-in is indicative of stiffness and a lack of suppleness which affects balance.

### SOLUTIONS: THE RIDER

a  If the horse is falling-in, there may be a fault in the rider's aiding.

- ◆ Check the inside leg position. If it is too far back, the horse cannot feel enough difference between the inside and outside leg, thus not understanding that a bend is required. We cannot create and control a bend with only one leg aid. The horse needs to feel the presence of the inside leg at the girth and the outside leg one or two hand widths behind it.

- ◆ If the outside leg is too active, it can confuse the horse into moving away from it, so wrongly applied aids can cause falling-in.

- ◆ The outside leg is normally passive, resting lightly on the horse's side on 'guard duty' to prevent the haunches evading the bend by swinging outwards. If the rider feels the horse attempting this evasion, the outside leg becomes active until the haunches are under control, then the leg reverts to its passive role.

- ◆ If the rider grips the saddle tightly with the knee, the leg aid can be ineffective and the horse may fall-in. The trainer must help the rider to relax the knee with some stretching exercises. The aim is that the leg should appear still, but without tightness. We want body tone but not tension.

- ◆ Lift and stretch the leg away from the saddle so there is daylight showing and then gently place it around the horse. Repeat a few times. This helps to break the grip and gives the draped quality we look for.

**b** If the rider makes the mistake of trying to steer by pulling the inside rein, it can cause the horse to fall-in, as he leans on the rein for support.

◆ Correct this by making the inside rein lighter. Think of how you would ride the circle if you had no inside rein. You would have to emphasise the outside aids for turning, plus the weight aid to the inside seat bone and the inside leg for bend and impulsion. The horse should remain upright on turns and circles rather than lean over like a motorcycle, and this requires an inside bend.

◆ A stiff horse that is falling-in is uses the rider's hands to lean on. When we soften the reins we deny him that crutch, so we must support him with our leg and seat aids. The intention is to help the horse find a better balance through bending and suppling exercises, so that eventually it is possible for him to find it a measure of self-carriage.

**c** If lack of suppleness is the cause of falling-in, we need to use some exercises to improve this.

Some may regard a horse that falls in as 'not obedient to the inside leg'. However if he is too stiff to move away from the leg, he is not being disobedient, but is physically unable to comply. He needs to be made looser before he can be 'obedient to the leg'.

## SUGGESTED EXERCISES

**1** Spiralling from a large circle to a small one is a good starting point; how small will depend on the degree of stiffness. Begin with 20m and gradually spiral in until 10m can be achieved without loss of balance, rhythm or outline. This is a gradual process and should be practised on both reins. Take care to offer the horse small yields on the inside rein during the spiral so that you help him find his balance through bending his body rather than allowing him to lean on the reins for support.

**2** Curved lines such as shallow loops (single serpentines) 5m or 10m in from the track are useful. They require the horse to make easy bending and straightening moves.

**3** Ride serpentines, commonly of three, four or five loops, each one touching the sides of the arena. Again these require several changes of bend linked by a few steps of straightness. These elements are the building blocks of all our training – a mixture of straight and curved lines. The rider must take care that these figures are performed maintaining balance and alignment at all times, otherwise the exercise is meaningless.

*right* In the first diagram the rider is on the left rein and rides a deep corner with left bending, then straightens the horse, changes bend opposite B, straightens the horse once more, then bends left for the corner. Riding the loop in this way provides gentle suppling work for the horse.

*far right* This is more demanding than the shallow loop as the degree of bend required is greater. In the 60m arena each loop is 15m and should be symmetrical. The horse should cross the centre line at 90 degrees, to ensure straightness is achieved, before starting the new bend of the next loop.

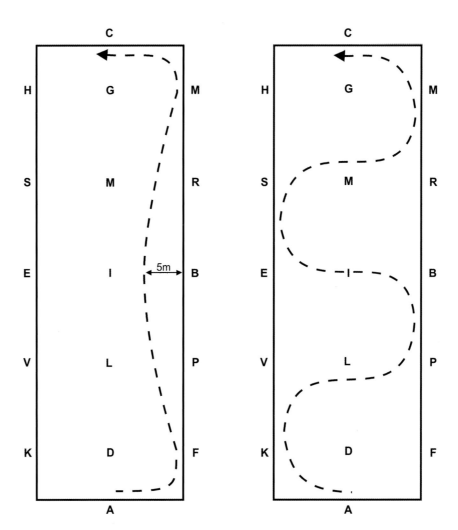

**d** Falling-in is usually most obvious when riding the canter. The extra momentum in canter will tend to push the stiff horse more onto his shoulders, aggravating the problem.

## SUGGESTED EXERCISES

**1** A useful exercise is to start from the centre line at A or C, and canter a diagonal line outwards to the corner marker (for example from A to H on the right rein, or A to M on the left. As you ride this line, use the inside leg to ask for bend at the ribcage, whilst maintaining a slight positioning of the head and neck to the inside.

   ◆ Take care with your seat aids that the speed does not increase, (or balance will be compromised) and by offering small forward yields of the rein on the stiff side, encourage the horse to relax and accept the contact more softly. Note that in this exercise you are not trying to create sideways steps; it is an exercise to improve the horse's balance and obedience to the leg aid.

♦ Remember to sit upright in the saddle, otherwise the seat aid will be ineffective and the horse will lean on his forehand. Rock the pelvis in slow motion to control the tempo, freeing the hands from being the 'brakes'.

2 Another simple canter exercise is to spiral down from a large to a small circle, then carefully use the inside leg to push your horse back out to a large one. Again the seat aids are important to help maintain balance and the rider should remember to make any half-halts brief; it is a mistake to hang on to the reins if the horse feels heavy. He will never become lighter if the rider tries to hold the horse with his hands.

♦ As you spiral out to the large circle, think of applying the aids in the same way as for the diagonal line exercise mentioned above. In both exercises the goal is the same – to improve suppleness and balance by creating a bend in the body, whilst controlling speed with the seat and encouraging the horse to relax his top line and seek the bit evenly.

♦ A deep seat that anchors the speed, combined with the legs to bend the horse's torso, and considerate hands that make discreet half-halts and yields is the correct way to gradually bring the horse into balance and deal with falling-in.

3 We can use lateral work to improve our horse's suppleness. Riding leg-yield can be an effective way to get the horse 'off' our leg; in other words, when a stiff horse leans his body against the leg aid and falls inwards, we can use the leg-yield to counter this.

♦ Let us assume that the horse is stiff to the left and falls in. This means he will feel hard and stiff to the inside (left) contact and too light in the outside (right) rein, caused by not stretching forwards to meet the bit correctly on that side.

♦ If we apply our inside leg (the left) at the girth, we can push our horse towards the outside rein (right) to create a slight bend around our inside leg. This reduces the weight in the inside hand and put the horse a little more into the outside contact.

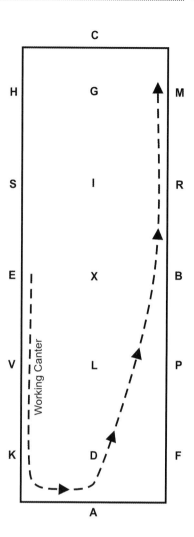

Working canter leg-yield: this exercise, sometimes known as a 'plié', is a useful method of softening the horse through his ribcage, therefore improving his balance in the canter. Unlike leg-yield in walk or trot, no crossing steps are required.

leans his weight onto the outside shoulder to evade supporting it with the weaker inside leg.

The rider may also feel through his seat that the inside hind leg does not take as big a step as the outside. When the horse is straight and both hind legs work evenly, both seat bones should alternately be lifted up and forward equally.

## SOLUTIONS

Imagine that you are riding a 20m circle and the horse bulges outwards, creating an oval shape. Check how much neck bend there is. You should only be able to see the corner of the inside eye. If you can see more than this, it is likely that the horse will be leaning his weight onto the outside shoulder and falling out.

- The solution is to reduce the excess inside neck bend, until the inside eye is just visible, and to support the horse better with the outside aids.

- A correct head and neck position will have the muzzle aligned with the centre of the horse's chest.

- Then align the forehand so that it is directly in front of the corresponding hind legs, taking care to monitor the feeling so that the horse does not revert back to being crooked.

- It is important that we remain sitting correctly on the circle and do not allow the horse to push our seat away from the inside hindquarter, which he may try to do to avoid carrying the rider on his weaker side.

- Check that you are not creating the problem by being too strong with the inside hand.

- If lightening the inside hand does not straighten the neck, then make soft half-halts to the outside rein, whilst using the inside leg to ask the inside hind leg to step more under the body and support the horse's own weight.

- The hand must not pull back towards the rider's body, but rather it remains positioned over the withers whilst it makes the aid, with the rider's leg pushing the horse towards the bit, not the hands pulling the bit towards the rider.

- This is a very important point for riders to take on board. A trainer has a duty to point out areas that need correcting, but it is the rider's responsibility to carry them out.

◆ If the rider pulls the outside rein to straighten the neck, the result will be that the horse braces his neck muscles against the rider, and the contact becomes even harder. We should always remember that we cannot straighten a horse by focusing on the head and neck alone; we have to address the whole horse.

◆ Note the outside leg which is normally passive, becomes active as a deterrent to drifting outwards.

## SUGGESTED EXERCISES

To improve the horse's response to the outside aids.

1  Example – assume the horse is crooked to the right. Walk or trot a 20m circle on the right rein and then gradually spiral smaller to 10 m, with a slight outside positioning in his body.

◆ Your left leg and rein are *temporarily* the inside aids as you adopt position left with your body. You guide the horse onto the diminishing circle by pressing him inwards with the left leg to create a better contact to your right rein, thereby encouraging an even contact. When you are on the 10m circle, carefully resume normal inside positioning and ride gradually out to a 20m circle. This simple exercise is very helpful in straightening the horse and ensures he listens to your outside aids.

2  Use leg-yield to better connect the horse with his soft or hollow side. Again, if he is hollow to the right, leg-yielding from left leg towards the right will assist the rider in creating a straighter, better balanced horse.

◆ This can be done from line to line, across the diagonal, or along the wall.

## SUGGESTED EXERCISES FOR STRAIGHTENING

Lateral work is very helpful when we are dealing with crookedness and falling-out. The idea is that we ask the horse to bend a little more towards his stiff side for a few steps, so that when we ride him once more in a correct bend, he will find it easier.

An example might be that our horse is curling to the right; his head and neck are too far to the inside and he carries the hindquarters to the inside. He falls out on turns and circles.

1  We can ride on an inside track and ask for a shoulder-out. (i.e. a shoulder-in left whilst on the right rein. After a few steps we can straighten him by bringing the forehand in line with the haunches. This exercise can be repeated a number

of times to improve mobility and, by allowing him to straighten in between episodes of shoulder-out, we can avoid tiring the weaker side.

◆ This can be ridden either on a straight line or a large circle.

2 Haunches-in (travers) and haunches-out (renvers) are also helpful when working with the crooked horse. Both of these exercises call for the horse to step laterally

*below left* Notice that when riding these exercises on the inside track, the rider must take care to maintain a straight line and not allow the horse to wander.
1. haunches-in (travers)
2. haunches-out (renvers),
3. shoulder-out.

*below right* The rider changes his seat, leg and rein aids to move from travers to shoulder-out, but the horse's positioning remains the same; only his bend changes. The subtle change of the weight aid this produces is very important as it helps the horse keep his balance during the exercise.

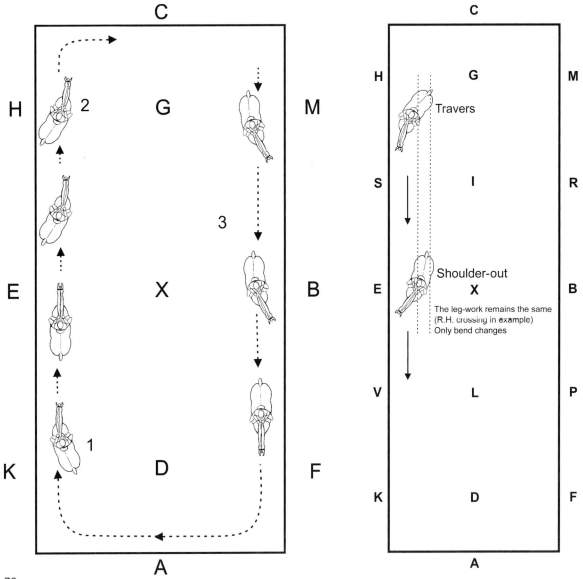

into the direction of bending and so are more demanding than shoulder-in with regard to balance and engagement.

♦ On an inside track, ask for few steps of haunches-in, straighten, then haunches-out. Check that the speed and rhythm remain the same.

The idea with a crooked horse is to create a feeling of evenness on both sides of his body. A horse which curls to the right will benefit from haunches-in on the left rein and haunches-out on the right rein (and vice versa for a horse that curls to the left).

♦ Always work exercises equally on both reins to develop an ambidextrous horse. It is important that with both haunches-in and haunches-out, that the rider *bends* the horse around the inside leg, otherwise it is no more than an accidental leg-yield, which will not give us the level of suppleness and engagement that we are looking for.

NB See Chapter 5 for details of the aiding for these lateral exercises.

**3** A helpful exercise is to ride shoulder-in, then change the bend and ride haunches-out. The positioning of the horse remains the same as does the leg, making the lateral, crossing step. Only the horse's bend changes.

**4** Alternately, we can ask for haunches-in then switch to shoulder-out. Again, only the bend changes; the crossing hind leg remains the same. That is, in haunches-in right, the left hind leg makes the crossing over step, and then in the shoulder-out left, it is still the left hind that crosses.

Both of these exercises require obedience and balance from the horse, in addition to developing his suppleness and therefore both are very useful when straightening a crooked horse.

**5** A further variation is to base the exercise on a figure-of-eight. For example, begin on a 20m circle, right rein. Ride haunches-in until the centre line at X then, keeping the haunches to the right, change onto a 20m circle left. The horse will now be performing haunches-out (renvers) on the left circle. Note that as before, the same hind leg is making the crossing steps.

♦ On returning to the centre line at X ride the right circle and once more the horse will be performing haunches-in.

♦ This of course should be ridden in both directions. If you or your horse is unfamiliar with the exercise, try it in walk a few times before moving on to the trot. See diagram overleaf.

1. The horse is asked for left travers on a 20m circle.

2. At X the rider changes rein to a right circle, but keeps the horse in the same positioning, so that it becomes a renvers on a right circle.

3. On returning to X the rider changes rein to make a left circle, again maintaining the same positioning, thus becoming a left travers once more. It will be found that after the renvers on the circle, the travers now feels much easier.

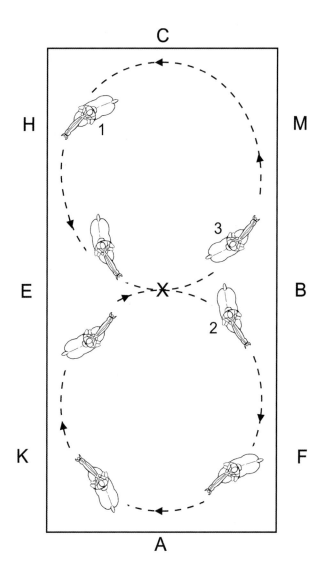

## The crooked canter

◆ Crookedness is most often seen at the canter, because unlike trot where the legs move in diagonal pairs, the asymmetrical motion of the canter gives a natural bias towards carrying the quarters to one side

◆ In order to develop the horse evenly on both reins, we need to correct this tendency, otherwise the horse will become very stiff on one rein and hollow on the other.

◆ A correct canter should have a slight bend through the whole horse from tail to poll, towards the leading leg.

For the horse to be straight in canter, it is necessary to bring the forehand slightly to the inside, so that the forefeet align with the corresponding hind feet.

- As horses are narrower at the shoulders than at their hips, it may be necessary to canter in shoulder-fore position to produce straightness. We should keep the muzzle lined up with the centre of the horse's chest, both on straight and curved lines, and bring the forehand slightly to the inside without allowing the neck to curl to either side.

- This means the inside hind leg cannot evade bearing weight, so shoulder-fore helps both in straightening and strengthening the horse.

## SHOULDER-FORE

◆ To ride the shoulder-fore, the rider sits with inside positioning. (See chapter on The Seat for explanation.)

◆ This brings the outside rein to touch the outside of the horse's neck and withers and is used as an indirect rein to move the shoulders slightly to the inside, about the width of one horseshoe. Note this is more of an inward feel by the rider, not a backward pull on the rein. With the outside rein, check that the neck remains straight.

◆ The inside rein keeps a light contact. We cannot create a shoulder-fore by pulling the inside rein. This would make the crookedness worse as the horse would bend the *neck* inwards excessively rather than moving the *shoulders* inwards.

◆ Stretching down into the inside stirrup keeps your weight to the inside seat bone and this helps the horse to maintain the shoulder-fore position under the centre of the rider's bodyweight; a rider who collapses a hip or moves around in the saddle will cause the horse to lose balance, and straightness will be lost.

◆ The inside leg aids at the girth to keep the haunches at the track and to maintain the canter.

◆ The outside leg behind the girth is passive, but is ready to correct any falling out from the haunches.

## Counter-canter

This is choosing to canter on the outside lead and is very helpful when dealing with crookedness. It helps because the horse is encouraged to straighten his body to deal with cantering 'in the wrong direction'. It will also improve his balance and suppleness, two important factors in straightening your horse. See Chapter 6 for further details on counter-canter

### SUGGESTED EXERCISES

◆ We can start counter-canter as a shallow loop/single serpentine of 3–5m deep. Use soft half-halts to ride a well-balanced canter with deep corners, so that the beginning of the loop is easier for your horse.

◆ Maintain your seat, leg and rein positions throughout the loop. If you shift your weight or try to steer the horse back to the track by pulling the outside rein, you can cause him to break to trot or to go dis-united. Instead, think of pushing him back to the track with the inside leg at the girth, at the same time ensuring he moves on a single track, and *not* on two tracks like a leg-yield.

◆ Try to stay relaxed; if you become tense in your body you will not be able to aid effectively and you will make him tense too.

◆ It is equally important not to pull if your horse feels unbalanced; he is likely to pull back and make the situation worse.

◆ When the counter-canter loop feels more balanced, progress onto riding a 15m half-circle at the end of the long side, returning to the track after the half marker. You can then ride a few counter-canter strides on the track until the corner marker, where you can make a trot transition.

◆ Gradually try to remain in counter-canter for longer, until you can ride the short end of the arena without breaking. If this is a problem, change the exercise to riding a 20m half-circle at B or E. Sometimes horses feel a little more confident at attempting the counter-canter if you ride it in the middle of the arena where he has more space, rather than close to the short end wall.

When the horse can perform a 20m circle or half-circle confidently in counter-canter, test his balance for self carriage by giving and retaking the reins as you cross the centre line.

*Try to stay relaxed; if you become tense in your body you will not be able to aid effectively…*

◆ Prepare for this by making a half-halt, then smoothly push your hands forwards towards the horse's ears until the reins are slack, and then gently return your hands to hold the reins in contact again over the withers. Two or three seconds is the approximate time to take over this. If the counter-canter is good, he should be able to maintain his rhythm and balance until you re-take the reins.

◆ It is important that the rider stays sitting down as he does this; the horse will need the support of the seat aid when the reins are given, otherwise he may fall onto his forehand.

◆ If the horse does not feel entirely balanced in the counter-canter, then you can build up to the give and re-take by yielding one rein at a time and then progress onto both when the horse has relaxed a little more.

◆ When riding counter-canter along the track, keep the horse's inside shoulder (i.e. on the inside of his bend) as close to the wall as possible, and the neck bend towards the leading leg to a minimum. This will help to keep the horse straight.

◆ We can finish the counter-canter by riding across the diagonal to resume true canter on the opposite wall, or by making a downward transition. It is better to make the transition away from a corner, so that the horse does not begin to anticipate a transition every time he approaches a corner in counter-canter.

## 5. Runs from the leg/on the forehand

A horse that runs from the leg overreacts to the rider's pushing aids and rushes forward and he will be on his shoulders.

A horse naturally carries around 60 per cent of his weight on his forehand because of the heavy head and neck. If we leave him in this state he will always work on his forehand. Our aim is to train him to transfer weight back to the haunches so that it is at least 50/50.

### Examples

**a** The horse could be nervous and lacking confidence, therefore runs from the thing that worries him; in this case the rider's leg aid.

**b** Or he may be out of balance and not in full control of his own body's responses.

**c** If he is excited, his responses may be heightened to the point where he does not really listen to the aids.

**d** Running often results in the horse being on his forehand.

**e** Conformation can be a factor.

**f** Physical stiffness can put the horse on his forehand.

### SOLUTIONS

**a** If the horse is very sensitive, he may be scared by a strong leg aid, causing him to run from the leg.

- Reduce the aid to a much lighter touch, ceasing the *instant* the horse responds. It will probably take time for the horse to gain confidence in the aids, and until then it is very important to remain patient and consistent in order to earn the horse's trust.

- Sharp spurs can also be to blame. Either ride without them or, if required under the rules of a competition, use a round-ended variety. Spurs are worn as a refinement to the leg aid, not to scare him into moving. They ought to deliver light, precise touches to the horse's sides from a still leg. A flapping leg armed with a spur is a dangerous thing!

**b** A horse may run from the leg aid because he lacks balance.

♦ Imagine that you start to run down a hill. Very soon you pick up speed and the added momentum makes it difficult to slow down or stop. When a horse is out of balance, it is likely he will experience a similar feeling of falling forward onto his forehand, at speed. Fortunately, because a horse has four legs, he rarely trips over.

♦ When the unbalanced horse feels the leg aid, it can produce a sensation of freefall onto his shoulder with little control of his own speed. The rider needs to slow down until the horse can find his equilibrium and can carry the weight more evenly between hindquarters and forehand. When this has been achieved through correct, soft half-halts, the responses to the pushing aids can be less extreme so that the horse can be ridden 'on the aids'.

**c** If the horse is over-excited, then we must ask why. Is he being fed appropriately; that is according to the amount of work he is getting, his size, age and temperament?

♦ For example some horses are naturally 'hot' and need feed that has slow release energy in order to work calmly.

♦ Other horses require working twice a day, in order for them to be attentive to the aids.

♦ If the high spirits are caused by a short break from work, then lungeing the horse before riding can help.

♦ It follows that, in all these instances, a composed, confident rider will help calm an excitable horse, so that he can be brought to a condition where he will listen properly to the aids.

If our horse is tense or over-excited, we have to relax his mind by working on his body. We do this by using various exercises to gradually loosen up his body so that he will then be in a state to listen to us. This does not mean that we aim to exhaust him; instead our training should maintain enough energy for him to be expressive in his work.

♦ Ride numerous transitions on circles, both between and within the gaits. The aim is to slow the horse down so he listens to our restraining seat and rein aids, whilst prompting him from our leg to step forward with controlled energy. Be tactful with the leg, otherwise we will accidentally push the horse onto his forehand.

- Frequent transitions will gain the horse's attention until he is ready to respond more calmly to our requests.

- For example, alternate six or eight trot steps with six or eight walk steps. If on a circle, the bend will help put the inside hind leg under the horse's weight and assist with balance.

- Ride the transitions on both reins and eventually on straight lines too, so that we have the horse on our seat aids. This can prevent him running onto his shoulders.

**d** When a horse is out of balance longitudinally, he will be inclined to run onto his forehand. If he is then driven strongly forwards, it will make him worse. The rider will feel the horse leaning on the bit and he will not be easy to turn or slow down.

- A horse that has weak hindquarters may naturally fall onto his forehand. This is because he does not have the strength to hold himself in balance, so he uses the hind legs to propel himself rather than carry weight.

- The rider must have a programme to strengthen the haunches over time to rectify this. This should include lateral work, transitions and possibly gymnastic jumping.

- During this work we must pay attention to riding the horse in good balance and gradually improving his ability to carry weight on the haunches with a swinging back.

**e** Conformation can play a part in this problem. A horse that is built with a large head and short, low-set-on neck will be loaded onto his forehand by nature. Equally, if a horse's hind legs are naturally out behind his hindquarters, it will predispose him to go on his shoulders.

*Spend time at the walk, to teach the horse to listen to your slowing aids.*

- Watch the hind leg action; it should not push out behind or snatch upwards. The hind toe should move forward and upward before being placed on the ground well under the horse's belly, where it can support weight.

- A horse that is croup-high will tend to have 'downhill' paces and a horse with a heavily built forehand will have to make more effort than the horse which is blessed with ideal conformation. Therefore we need to be careful when training to overcome these disadvantages and find better balance.

- Spend time at the walk, to teach the horse to listen to your slowing aids. The walk is easier to control than the other gaits and the horse is less likely to escape by picking up speed and leaning onto his shoulders. We should focus on creating a good connection from hocks to bridle so that the horse is through his back. This is essential if the horse is to be able to transfer weight from his forehand back to the haunches.

◆ Correctly ridden half-halts are essential to improve the horse's ability to find a better balance. Riding these transitions on a circle instead of straight lines is a helpful way to start this work.

◆ If the horse ignores the half-halt, make a halt transition instead. Ensure that he stands immobile before you ask him to move off rather than allowing him to drift forward. We need the horse to listen to our restraining seat aids so that we are not tempted to over-use our hands when the horse wants to lean on the reins for support.

**f** A horse that is tense or stiff in his back may also run onto his forehand. Ride many transitions both between the paces and within them to supple him.

◆ Try riding canter-trot-canter transitions on a 20m circle. Ride one half in trot and then the second half in canter. When his balance improves, ride fewer strides in canter before making the trot transition. The frequent changes from the two-beat trot to the three-beat canter can help to soften the horse's back.

◆ We can also use cavalletti and ground poles when working to improve a stiff back. The extra effort made by the horse to step over the poles or cavalletti will encourage greater flexibility in the hips and hind leg joints.

## Pole work

It is useful to have an assistant with you for this work, to set out and adjust the equipment as necessary. For safety it is recommended to use cavalletti on their lowest setting, or secure the poles in blocks so that they cannot roll and trip the horse.

### SUGGESTED EXERCISE

◆ If the horse is unfamiliar with pole work, begin by walking over a single pole from both reins. Make sure you ride over the centre of the pole and that you meet it straight.

- When the horse is going calmly, progress onto trotting over the single pole, again on both reins.

- An average distance between poles set for trot work is 1.3m.

- An average distance for walk is 0.9m.

- Proceed to three poles, but if the horse shows signs of trying to jump them, either return to the single pole until he is calm, or you can double the distance between the poles to develop his confidence when he sees a line of poles in front of him.

- When you are satisfied that your horse is confident doing this, then build up to a line of five or six poles.

- The exercise can be varied by arranging the poles in a fan pattern. Keep the standard distance for the middle of each pole and then you have the option of lengthening the stride by riding a little to the outside of centre, or shortening the stride by riding to the inside of centre.

- Using raised poles or cavalletti on their lowest height will encourage the horse to articulate his joints more to give rounder steps. Take care to keep the horse calm and do not let him rush the exercise.

- The distance between poles may vary slightly according to the size of the horse and his stride length, so your assistant can make any adjustments to the distances to best suit the horse's stride.

- When the horse can negotiate the poles calmly and in a good even rhythm, you can raise the cavalletti to the middle height and ask the horse to trot with greater lift in his stride.

See pole work exercises diagram opposite.

## 6. Turning difficulties

- A stiff horse may lean onto his forehand, making steering difficult. The ability to turn left and right without either drifting out or falling in is fundamental.

- However it is possible that turning is uncomfortable due to an ill-fitting bit or sharp teeth on one side of his jaw. This is more of a stable management question rather than training, but should be addressed at the first opportunity.

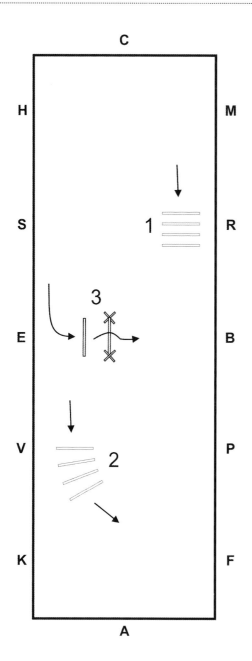

This is a small sample of possible exercises using ground poles or cavalletti.

1. The poles are arranged off the track to allow full use of the width of the arena when working around the poles. Space them approximately 1.3m apart for trot or 0.9m when in walk.

2. The fan pattern allows the rider to vary the length of the stride according to where the pole is crossed. It is also a good test of accuracy and being able to maintain a chosen line when turning. In both exercise 1 and 2, the poles may be raised at one or both ends. This asks the horse to articulate his joints to a greater extent to improve suppleness and looseness.

3. This exercise has a small jump (0.6–0.8m high) with a placing pole in front. If you wish to approach in canter, allow a 5 or 6m, or from trot, 2.6 to 3m distance.

Note that if you wish to ride a grid of cavelletti at canter, a normal one-stride distance is 6m, two strides 10m and no stride (a bounce) 3.5m. It is important to adjust the distances to suit the individual horse. The idea is to give him some fun and help improve him gymnastically, not to trick him.

◆ Work on a combination of large (20m) circles and straight lines. The aim is that the horse listens to our leg aids and that we can gradually supple him so that he can bend his body and neck to match the curve of the circle he makes in the arena. Straightness is vital if we are going to progress our horse's training.

◆ Serpentines in three or more loops will also improve the horse's reactions to the turning aids.

## WHY DOES THIS MATTER?

If the head is tilted there is no longer an even contact on both sides of the bit. If we do not pay attention to this problem, it can become very difficult to cure, as the horse will learn that he can avoid the action of the bit by locking his poll and tilting the head. It impacts on the willing submission to the bit that is necessary for us to train properly; but it is a bad habit made by the rider, not the horse.

## SOLUTIONS

a The most common cause of head tilting is that one rein is stronger than the other. So if the right hand is too strong, we could see that the muzzle tilts up to the right and the left ear drops lower.

◆ The answer is to soften the right hand, thus making the horse comfortable in his mouth and encouraging him to relax once again.

b Occasionally the head tilt is due to a medical problem such as a tooth abscess, or pain in the poll area affecting the axis and atlas joints. Equally a fall or becoming cast in his stable could lead to a condition that leads to head tilting. If any of these cases are suspected, then consult the veterinary surgeon for advice on how to proceed with treatment.

## 9. Teeth grinding

We want our horse to work with a relaxed jaw, so that we have an even contact that has an elastic quality. If he grinds his teeth it indicates that he is generally tense, or uncomfortable in his mouth.

Teeth grinding will also be marked down in competition, as a sign of contact problems, or tension, and that willing submission is not what it should be.

## SOLUTIONS

a It can be caused by the rider taking too strong a contact on the reins, and the horse shows his discomfort by grinding his teeth. Here the trainer must help the rider establish a lighter feel on the horse's mouth. This may indicate that there are problems in the seat that need to be addressed.

◆ If the horse is strong, then the rider needs to use his seat aids more effectively instead of pulling harder on the reins. It may be that he needs to improve his balance in the saddle so that he is independent of the reins. (See chapter on 'The Seat' for further explanation.)

b It can be the result of asking the horse for something that is too difficult for him, causing nervous tension. For example, demanding too much collection before the horse is strong enough in the haunches. Here the answer could be to ask for collection for a shorter period, and then perhaps some stretching to relax mind and body before returning to the collected work.

Although we do need to ask the horse for more difficult exercises if we are to progress his training, this must be done with tact and understanding.

c With nervous horses, one can sometimes notice teeth grinding when a new exercise is introduced. However, when they understand and become familiar with it, they relax and the grinding stops.

Again the rider should be sympathetic and proceed with discretion. The aids must be clear and given with good timing and feel. A good rider is always prepared to 'correct back' a stage in order for the horse to understand and feel confident in his work.

For example, suppose your horse is becoming tense when you introduce flying changes; he grinds his teeth and pulls. It may be that he does not understand your aids, especially if you are not very experienced. It would be sensible to return to simple changes; allowing both horse and rider time to find harmony again. When this is secure, the flying changes can be reintroduced.

> *A good rider is always prepared to 'correct back' a stage in order for the horse to understand and feel confident in his work.*

d Teeth grinding may be caused by pain from sharp teeth which can cut the inside of the cheek or cause an ulcer. Your veterinary surgeon or equine dentist can advise you on this and any action required.

e An ill-fitting saddle or noseband can also lead to teeth grinding. A drop or flash noseband should only be tightened enough to stop the horse from opening and crossing his jaw, which can be a bad habit of young horses. It also prevents the mouth opening to evade poll flexion. It should not be so tight that it prevents the horse from working comfortably with a relaxed jaw.

The saddle can cause pain if it presses on the withers, does not have a clear channel above the spine, exerts pressure under the points of the saddle, or is too narrow and pinches.

A broken or damaged tree can likewise cause problems and needs to be rectified before the saddle is used again. Incorrectly flocked panels can be a problem causing pressure points and any of the issues listed could lead to teeth grinding. A qualified saddler needs to be consulted to effect repairs or even to change the saddle altogether.

In summary, the causes of teeth grinding may not be straightforward and, if this is the case, seek advice from an experienced trainer to offer guidance as to the best course of action.

# 5

# LATERAL WORK PROBLEMS

## TURN ON THE FOREHAND

### Purpose

◆ A turn on the forehand is a basic movement designed to teach a young horse to move away from the leg.

◆ It also has value in introducing the concept of lateral work to a novice rider.

◆ As it is performed at the halt, it has little gymnastic value. Once the movement is understood, we should progress onwards and not practise it too often.

### Aids for turn on the forehand

◆ Make a square halt, with the horse remaining attentively on the aids.

◆ Use the inside rein to flex the horse slightly away from the direction of the turn.

◆ The inside leg, at the girth (or slightly behind, if the horse does not understand) quietly pushes the hindquarters away so that the inside hind leg crosses in front of the outside hind leg. Try to control each step so that the horse does not rush.

◆ The rider remains tall in the saddle and the outside rein maintains soft contact so that the horse does not move forward during the turn; he should pivot around the inside foreleg.

- The rider's outside leg is kept at the girth to ensure the horse does not step back during the turn.

- It is usual to execute the turn as a quarter (90 degrees) or half (180 degrees) turn on the forehand.

# PROBLEMS WITH TURN ON THE FOREHAND

## 1. Moves forward during the turn

During the turn the horse may push forward rather than pivoting around his inside foreleg.

### SOLUTIONS

**a** This may happen because the young horse does not understand that you want him to move away from the leg.

- Usually turn on the forehand is the introduction to lateral work, and until then he has only been required to move forward when he feels a leg aid, so in fact he may be trying to please his rider when he makes this mistake.

- Be patient and take time for him to understand, so that he does not become tense. Repeat the aids quietly and only ask for one or two steps at first, then praise him and walk on to another place where you can ask again.

- Try halting facing the wall and close to it. This can deter the horse from stepping forwards.

*Be patient and take time for him to understand, so that he does not become tense.*

**b** However, it may be that he steps forward because the rider's outside rein is not maintaining a controlling contact. This does not mean you should pull, rather that you maintain the feel as if in a halt.

- When the inside leg is applied to ask the horse to move away, the horse's first reaction is to move forward. When he feels the outside rein does not yield to allow this, he takes the second option, which is to move sideways away from the leg pressure.

**c** If the rider tips forward in the saddle, the shift in bodyweight can be enough to unbalance the horse and cause him to step forward. It is important to sit still and not disturb him.

**d** The horse may step forward to evade crossing his inside hind leg.

◆ In this case it can be helpful to halt close to and facing the wall. The presence of the wall can deter him from walking forward and allow the rider to perform the turn without becoming stronger in the reins.

e  Stepping forward can also result in falling-out through the outside shoulder. The solution is to use the outside rein to limit the amount of neck bend. The more that is permitted, the more likely the horse is to escape through the outside shoulder. Do not forget that we want only a *small* flexion away from the direction of movement.

## 2. Moves backwards during the turn

The horse is required to pivot around the inside foreleg, not step backwards.

### SOLUTIONS

a  This fault may be due to the rein contact being too strong, causing the horse to step back. The trainer should remind the rider to keep a steady but light rein contact to give the horse confidence.

*... keep a steady but light rein contact to give the horse confidence.*

b  It may be that the rider's outside leg is not supporting the horse during the turn; it should 'hold' him in place as he is asked to pivot around the inside foreleg. There must be a balance between the sideways aid and the 'remain in place' aids.

## 3. Inside hind leg does not cross

During the turn on the forehand the inside hind leg should cross in front of the outside one, as in a leg-yield.

### SOLUTIONS

a  If the horse is lazy or lethargic, his inside hind leg can step next to, but not across, the outside hind. Try supporting the inside leg aid with a tap from the schooling whip.

◆ Alternatively, ride actively in trot or canter, then ride a square halt and ask for the movement. This can make the horse more responsive to your aids and produce the crossing step as required.

b  A stiff or weak horse may have difficulty in showing the crossing step. We can help him by altering the movement to a turn *around* the forehand.

◆ Instead of halting, then asking the hindquarters to move away, we *almost* halt, and then ask in the normal way. This makes it easier for the horse to mobilise his hindquarters and to make the inside hind cross in front of the outside one.

◆ The price we pay for the turn *around* the forehand is that the horse will move a little forward rather than pivot on the inside foreleg. We should regard this as a compromise in order to help supple the horse sufficiently so that he can then progress to the normal turn on the forehand.

## SUGGESTED EXERCISE

◆ Walk along the centre line. At G almost halt, then push the hindquarters around with the inside leg, taking care that, with soft half-halts from the outside rein, we limit the forward steps to a minimum, lest the turn becomes so large that he no longer crosses the inside hind leg. At D ask for another turn around the forehand. Repeat this manoeuvre on both reins until the horse starts to feel looser.

◆ An alternative exercise is to ride a 20m circle around X. Each time you get to the centre line on the circle, ask for the turn around the forehand, using the inside leg to push the hindquarters outwards until you have made a 180 degree turn and can then proceed on the circle on the other rein. On reaching the centre line for the second time, ask for another turn around the forehand, thereby changing rein once again.

> Note this exercise is equally suitable for turn *on* the forehand too.

c On occasion the inside hind leg may step across but *behind* the outside hind leg. Again we should check that the outside rein is not too strong and that there is enough outside leg on the horse for him to be *thinking* forwards rather than backwards.

d The preparation for this movement should include a square halt, with the horse remaining on the aids so that he is mentally and physically ready for whatever you ask for.

◆ Check the preparation. If the halt is not square, then it is difficult for any horse to perform the movement correctly. If the inside hind has halted behind the outside hind, then how is the horse to make the correct crossing step?

◆ Or if the horse is resting a hind leg, the rider should first square him by using the opposite leg to gently push the horse to stand on all four legs. We must begin with a straight halt and the weight evenly distributed over all four legs.

## 4. Horse throws head above the bit during the turn

The horse should remain on the aids during the turn on the forehand.

### SOLUTION

If we assume that the horse was on the bit prior to asking for the turn, then it is likely that the rider's hands are too strong and pulling on the bit. He must soften his contact and make rein aids with a vibrating effect, not a solid backward pull. The hands should remain in position above the withers, not end up closer to the rider's body.

# LEG-YIELD

## General

- As it does not require collection, leg-yield is suitable for young or green horses and is usually the first lateral movement to be taught that involves forward motion.

- He should move forwards and sideways with the inside limbs crossing in front of the outside ones.

- During leg-yield the horse should be practically straight, with only a slight flexion away from the direction of travel.

## Purpose

- To teach the horse to move laterally whilst maintaining rhythm and balance.

- It has some suppling benefits for the hindquarters and through the ribcage.

## Aids for leg-yield

- In leg-yield left from the centre line to the outside track, the horse would show a slight flexion towards the centre line and the rider's right rein and leg are the inside aids.

- The aim is to move forwards and sideways to the track with the horse almost parallel to the wall.

- First prepare the horse with a half-halt, then bring your inside shoulder a little back, bringing more weight onto the inside seat bone. The inside leg, at or very slightly behind the girth, pushes the horse sideways so that the inside fore and hind legs cross in front of the outside ones.

- The outside rein controls the neck positioning and the tempo through soft half-halts.

- The outside leg at the girth supports the horse and keeps the rhythm. With any lateral movement, the idea is to maintain the same speed and rhythm as when riding on a single track.

- The inside rein maintains the slight flexion away from the direction of movement with as light a feel as possible.

- Leg-yields can be ridden in walk, trot and in canter (here the legs do not cross) either along the wall, from line to line or from a small circle to larger one.

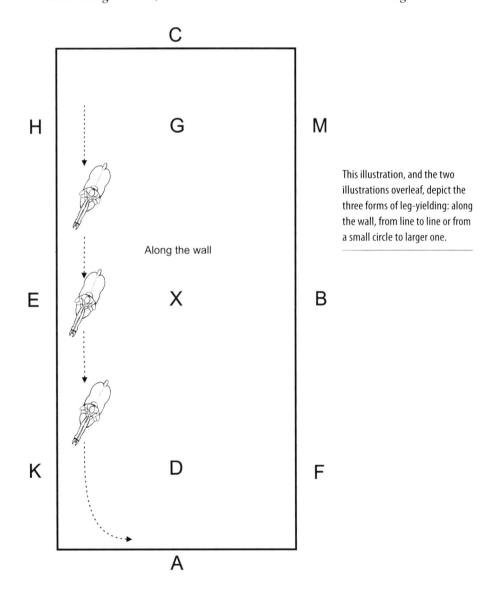

Along the wall

This illustration, and the two illustrations overleaf, depict the three forms of leg-yielding: along the wall, from line to line or from a small circle to larger one.

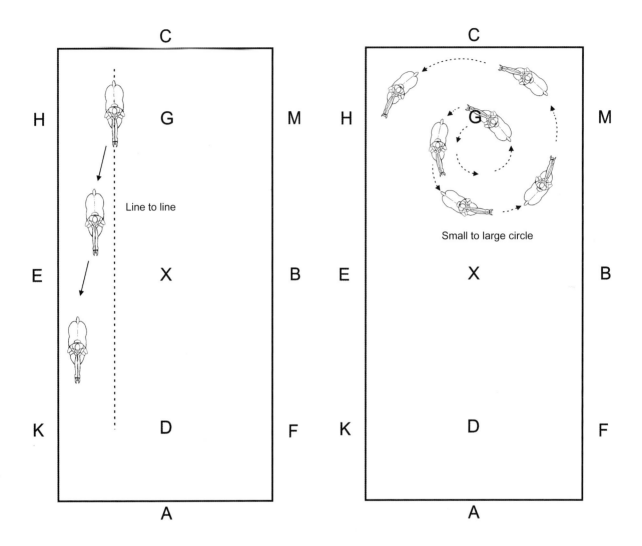

Line to line

Small to large circle

## PROBLEMS WITH LEG-YIELD

### 1. Does not move off the leg

#### SOLUTIONS

A sluggish response to the sideways aid may be a timing problem from the rider. The leg aid is most effective when applied just as the hind leg on the same side is about to leave the ground.

◆ If you have a problem with this, try to feel when your right seat bone is being pushed up and forward by the horse's right hind leg.

- This means that his right hind is in the air and about to *touch* the ground and the left hind leg is about to *leave* the ground. This is the moment to apply your left leg to influence the placement of the left hind leg.

- In other words, the horse can only respond to your leg aid when the corresponding hind leg is leaving the ground, not when it is on the floor!

A minimal reaction to the sideways aid can be because the horse is stiff laterally.

## SUGGESTED EXERCISES

- Try making the exercise easier by asking for fewer steps or by leg-yielding from a 10m circle out to a 20m circle. Moving towards the larger circle is easier for the horse and should encourage him to move away from your leg more readily.

- If you are performing the exercise along the wall, ask for a slight angle so that it is less demanding.

- It can also be helpful to ride the leg-yield in walk across the diagonal and when you reach the second three-quarter line, ride a half-turn *around* the forehand (see earlier) to deepen the crossing over steps, then leg-yield back almost to your starting point, then turn *around* the forehand once again and so on. A few repetitions of this on both reins should improve the depth of the crossing steps and loosen your horse's hindquarters.

- If he is generally sluggish, ride a series of up and down transitions to better bring him on to your aids.

## 2. Falls through outside shoulder

If the rider allows too much neck bend to the inside, then the horse will fall through his outside shoulder and there will be almost no crossing steps.

## SOLUTIONS

a  You may need to make short, repeated half-halts to the outside rein to maintain straightness in his neck and body; then the sideways steps will be genuinely adding to the suppling effect of the exercise.

- Keep the forward impulse so that the exercise is both *forwards* and sideways. If the activity is lost, the horse may fall sideways onto his shoulder and the leg-yield will be of no help.

**b** A crooked rider who collapses the inside hip can also cause the horse to fall onto the outside shoulder.

 ◆ Try to keep the inside shoulder up and back as you ride the leg yield and remember to stretch the inside leg downwards too. It is important that the rider's seat does not slide across the saddle to the outside, which would unbalance the horse.

## SHOULDER-IN

### General

 ◆ This is normally the next lateral exercise to be introduced. It is a two-track movement and, unlike leg-yield, there should be a uniform bend from tail to poll, around the rider's inside leg.

*Below and opposite page*
These pictures each show a correct shoulder-in using both snaffle and double bridles. The front views show that the horse's muzzle remains in line with the centre of his chest, whilst in the rear view the inside hind and outside forelegs are clearly on one line.

- The forehand is brought a little in from the track; the hind legs stay at the track.

- This creates a movement that is shown on three lines. (The inside foreleg makes the first line, then the inside hind leg and outside foreleg on the second line and finally the outside hind leg makes the third line.)

- If the horse is very supple, it can be ridden on four lines – but this is not required for competition.

- The muzzle should remain in line with the centre of the horse's chest.

- In training we can ride it on a straight line, or on a circle. This can be useful if the horse anticipates the shoulder-in along the track and tries to rush through the movement.

## Purpose

- To improve engagement of the inside hind leg.

- Lighten the forehand.

The shoulder-in on four lines demonstrates the horse's suppleness; but without the bend, it would merely be an accidental leg-yield.

◆ Gain control of the shoulders and thereby give the rider a tool with which to deal with crookedness.

◆ It is also a means of developing collection as the inside hind leg has to step well under the body and carry more weight.

◆ *Shoulder-fore* is a related movement, where there is a slight angle to the track, but no bend in the horse.

◆ It can be shown in walk, trot and canter.

## Aids for shoulder-in

◆ The rider's seat, leg and rein positions are the same as for riding a 10m circle; sit tall and create an inside bend by turning your upper body so your shoulders are parallel to the horse's shoulders. This brings the outside rein close to the outside of the neck at the withers.

◆ The inside leg is at the girth and pushes the horse sideways along the track and also maintains the impulsion.

◆ The outside leg is a little behind the girth in a passive role to prevent the hindquarters from escaping the bend by pushing outwards. If the rider feels the quarters *trying* to push out, then the outside leg becomes an active aid to correct this.

◆ The outside rein both controls the tempo and neck bend and helps to bring the forehand in from the track.

◆ The inside rein shows the inside neck position.

## PROBLEMS WITH SHOULDER-IN

### 1. Only the neck bends to the inside; forehand remains on the track

SOLUTIONS

**a** The problem may be too much inside rein. The forehand cannot be moved inwards by the inside rein alone. It is by a combination of seat, weight, legs and both reins; just as in a correctly ridden circle.

**b** If the rider surrenders the outside rein when the horse is not established in the shoulder-in, the result may be the hooves remain on the track and only the head and neck turns inwards. (When the horse is secure in shoulder-in, it should be possible to give and re-take either rein for a few steps to demonstrate self-carriage.) Until that time, the horse needs the support of the outside rein which both limits the neck bend and also helps to move the forehand inwards.

**c** The shoulder-in may begin well, but after a few steps, the rider loses control of the outside shoulder and the forehand drifts back on to the track. This is more likely when working on the horse's soft or crooked rein as the horse seeks to evade carrying weight on the weaker inside hind leg.

Only the neck bends to the inside; forehand remains on the track.

When working on the horse's crooked rein, it can happen that the horse pushes the rider to the outside to avoid carrying weight on his weaker hindquarter; but the rider must remain in the centre of the saddle, stretching down into the inside stirrup to keep the horse balanced under the centre of his weight.

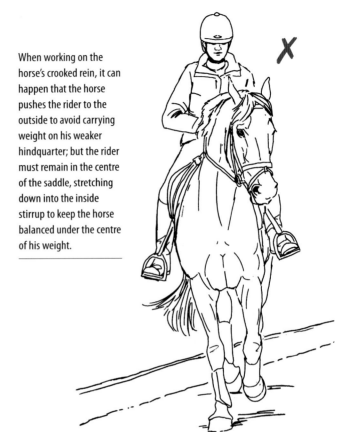

## 2. Rider slipping to the outside, angle varies

### SUGGESTED EXERCISES

◆ Ride shoulder-fore – that is, bring the forehand in maybe one horseshoe width from the track, but keep the horse straight. This will help you to keep the horse in balance and the forehand under control.

◆ A more advanced exercise is to ride some steps in renvers, then half-halt and change to shoulder-in. If control of the forehand is difficult, switch to renvers again and so on.

◆ The renvers improves the rider's influence over the positioning of the forehand and the inside shoulder. Of course when we change to the shoulder-in, the old inside shoulder becomes the new *outside* one, and the rider has a good opportunity to position the movement correctly with the horse in better balance.

## 3. Angle too wide

### SOLUTIONS

**a** This may be due to mistiming the preparatory half-halt at the start of the shoulder-in. If the movement has been set up by riding a 10m circle, then the half-halt should be given just *before* the horse completes the circle, so that the rider has time to use the inside leg to push the horse along the track with the horse at a slight angle only. If the half-halt is made *after* the horse finishes his 10m circle, then he will not have time to react and will likely think he is to embark on a second circle, so that when the shoulder-in aids are given, he will be on too wide an angle.

**b** A rider inexperienced in lateral work may misjudge the amount of angle and ask for too much causing the horse to lose balance and it possibly becomes a leg-yield by mistake.

**c** In a correct shoulder-in, the inside hind leg should step well under the horse's centre of gravity so that it engages and carries more weight. If the angle becomes

From revers to shoulder-in: these two photographs illustrate a good exercise for gaining control of the forehand during shoulder-in. It is also very good for improving obedience to the aids and demonstrating suppleness.

X

The level of suppleness will determine the amount of angle in the shoulder-in. A horse lacking suppleness should only be asked for a modest angle.

too wide the inside hind foot can step past the centre of gravity and be placed on the ground beyond the outside of the body, therefore losing its ability to support the haunches. In effect the horse will be falling sideways with the haunches accidentally out, rather than the shoulders being in from the track in a controlled and balanced way.

◆ In these situations, think of 'less is more' and ride a small angle. If you have arena mirrors, check that the outside foreleg is in line with the inside hind. If there are no mirrors, ask for 'good eyes on the ground' to help you learn the feeling.

d Sometimes the movement may begin well, but after a few steps it deteriorates, either becoming too wide, or the shoulders drift back to the wall.

◆ Frequently this is associated with an unbalanced rider who does not sit still with a supple back and deep seat. This can disturb the horse and create the situation where the angle of shoulder-in varies.

◆ The rider may benefit from rehearsing the movement in walk to co-ordinate his timing and aids so that the horse understands what is required.

◆ If however the trainer can see that it is the horse that struggles with balance, it can be the case that the rider is driving the trot too strongly at this moment. Here it can be helpful to slow down the trot temporarily, until balance, rhythm and throughness are restored. Again, riding a more modest angle will help.

## 4. The horse goes above the bit

### SOLUTIONS

a A common cause is the rider being too strong in the contact, which can be on one or both reins.

◆ Try half-halting, then giving and re-taking the rein on the side which feels strongest; if the horse relaxes and softens into the correct outline, he has told us that the rein was too strong!

**b** If the problem persists, we may be demanding too much angle or too many steps, especially if our horse is stiff or weak.

- In this case, ride a few shoulder-in steps with a milder angle then either make a 10m circle and reorganise his balance, softness and bend before continuing with more shoulder-in or, alternatively, after a few steps, ride across a diagonal and change the rein. This will give the horse a better chance of building his strength and suppleness without teaching him the *wrong* way to shoulder-in.

**c** A stiff rider who bumps in the saddle can lead to the horse becoming hollow and tense as a defence against the discomfort.

- Test this by riding rising trot. If the horse relaxes and works on the bit, then the rider is too stiff when sitting.

- The answer is to return to basics and correct the rider's seat. We need to swing in the lumbar spine area if we are to be properly seated and harmonious with the horse's motion. Only then can we expect the horse to be through his back and remain on the bit.

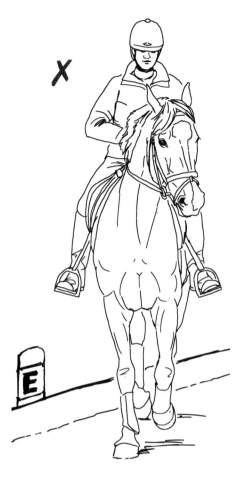

Here the horse goes above the bit in shoulder-in.

# TRAVERS/HAUNCHES-IN

## General

- This lateral movement fundamentally differs from shoulder-in and leg-yield because the horse is now required to move *and* bend in the same direction. This demands greater suppleness, bend and strength in the haunches.

- Although the outside hind leg makes the crossing step, it is the inside one which has to carry more weight, because the horse's and rider's combined weight is moved sideways over it.

- It is important that the horse bends all the joints of the hind legs and steps well under his body so that he is 'weight-lifting' thus building strength. If this does not happen, he will merely be sliding sideways with no gymnastic benefit.

- In travers, the outside hind leg moves slightly to the inside of the line made by the inside foreleg. The outside legs cross over in front of the inside ones.

These two examples of haunches-in are shown ridden in both snaffle and double bridles. They show that the forehand stays at the track with the horse's face parallel to the wall. The outside leg displaces the quarters inwards so that the horse moves with an inside bend on four lines. Notice that both riders sit with inside body positioning and that their shoulders remain level.

◆ This creates a movement which is on four lines.

◆ As with all lateral movements, finish by straightening the horse before you reach the next corner.

## Aids for travers

◆ It is easier to introduce the movement to both horse and rider in walk, although the gymnastic benefit occurs when performed in collected trot.

◆ The rider's seat, legs and reins are positioned as if for a 10m circle.

◆ Begin the travers either from a 10m circle, or immediately after a corner as you approach the long side of the arena.

104

- Ensure that your horse is relaxed, round and correctly on the aids.

- Make a half-halt to prepare your horse both physically and mentally for the travers.

- Position his head and neck so that he is looking straight ahead, with the outside of his face parallel to the wall. You should be looking between his ears to where you are going.

- Your inside leg remains at the girth so that you can maintain the speed and rhythm.

- The outside leg should be a little behind the girth to displace the haunches in from the track, so that he is bent around your inside leg.

- Sit with your shoulders parallel to the horse's shoulders and with slightly more weight on the inside seat bone.

> In other words, whenever we bend the horse, we always sit either position right for right bending or, position left for left bending. This applies to riding corners, circles or when we are bending the horse in a lateral movement, on straight or curved lines.
>
> It is also appropriate when riding in canter, as there will be a slight bend through the body towards the leading leg.

- Soft half-halts with the outside rein help to control the speed and the outside shoulder.

- After a few steps straighten up and ride out of the movement.

## PROBLEMS WITH TRAVERS/HAUNCHES-IN

### 1. The horse does not move off the leg

Of course this is not a problem confined to the travers, but is one of the basics in training. Nonetheless, when we first introduce a new lateral movement it can happen that there is some initial resistance to the leg aid.

#### SOLUTIONS

a If the horse seems inattentive, gain his attention by using your leg in an 'on-off' way. The repeating nature of the aid can make your wishes clearer to him.

♦ We can also give light touches with the schooling whip where the outside leg touches the horse to reinforce the aid.

**b** When introducing travers, make it easier by starting with a 10m circle as this gives the bend required for the movement.

♦ As you ride the 10m circle, apply a half-halt two steps before the circle is complete; then, as the forelegs reach the track but the haunches are still one step in from the track, ask with your outside leg to start the travers. As the horse is already in a travers position, this can make it straightforward for him to understand.

♦ Later, he should be obedient enough to start the travers from a straight line.

## 2. Too much neck bend

In travers the horse's head and neck should look straight down the track, with his face parallel to the wall. It is a common fault to over-use the inside rein and pull the head inwards, so that the horse is looking towards the centre line instead.

Besides being uncomfortable for the horse, it can block the progress of the inside foreleg and affect the rhythm.

### SOLUTION

The rider should lighten the contact on the reins and allow the horse to be both forwards and sideways. As ever, we wish the exercise to enhance the horse's paces, not break them down.

## 3. Angle too wide

With excessive angle, the hind legs can step too much sideways, beyond the horse's centre of gravity, thus the movement loses the function of improving engagement.

### SOLUTIONS

**a** This may be due to loss of energy (not enough forward activity rather than more speed). Here the rider must ensure that his inside leg aid is effective at the girth so that the balance between forwards and sideways movement is preserved.

**b** The outside rein should maintain an elastic contact, as one of its purposes is to control the degree of neck bend. If the neck is straighter and the horse is activated, the angle should reduce and the travers can be positioned correctly.

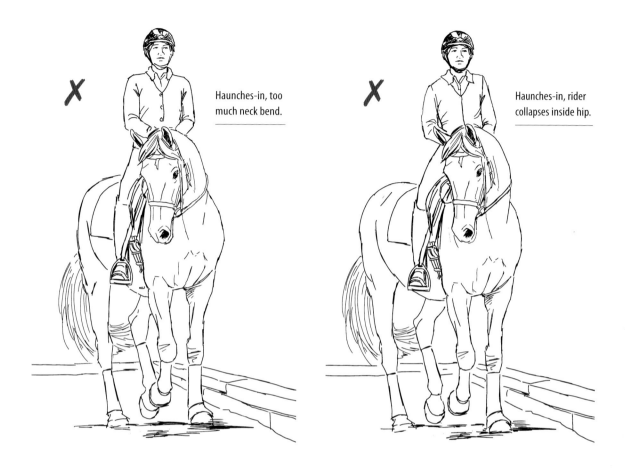

Haunches-in, too
much neck bend.

Haunches-in, rider
collapses inside hip.

## 4. Rider collapses seat/angle varies

When the horse's hind leg makes the crossing step, the outside hip will rise and fall more than normal and the rider must guard against sliding to the outside, especially if he is prone to drawing up the outside leg and collapsing the inside hip.

### SOLUTIONS

**a** Have a mental image of sitting more onto the inside seat bone to counter the possibility of sliding to the outside; this does not literally mean shift the seat bones across the saddle; just imagine it.

**b** The rider should be encouraged to sit tall in the saddle, keeping the inside collar-bone up and stretching down softly into the inside heel.

◆ The outside leg should be positioned behind the girth as if taking half a small step back with the leg from the hip, with the heel remaining the lowest point. This preserves more weight in the inside seat bone and stirrup.

- It is a mistake to take the outside leg back from the knee joint, as this lifts the outside heel and risks losing the stirrup iron, making the seat less secure.

- Working without stirrups would help improve the seat.

# RENVERS/HAUNCHES-OUT

## General

This movement, also known as tail to the wall, is like the mirror image of shoulder-in.

*below and opposite page*
Renvers is shown both in snaffle and double bridles and from in front and behind to show the correct position.

- Imagine shoulder-in right; the hind legs are on the track and the forehand is a little in on the second track. There is a bend around the rider's right leg. In renvers the horse's body positioning is the same, *except* that the horse is bent around the rider's left leg, which then becomes the inside one.

◆ When the forehand reaches the renvers position, continue back the way you have come along the track. During the whole sequence the bend remains the same, and most horses will find it easier to move into the renvers.

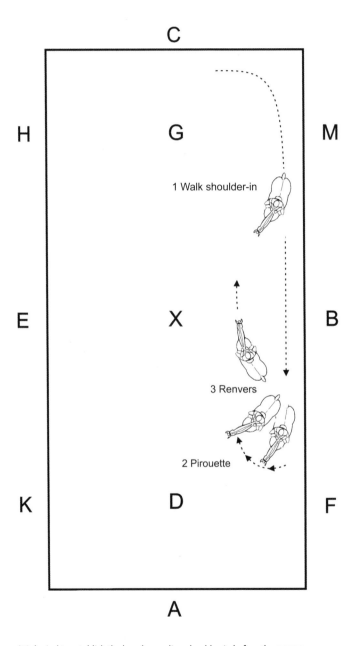

It is logical to establish the less demanding shoulder-in before the renvers. Then it can be used to prepare the renvers. The bend of the horse remains constant throughout the sequence and the walk pirouette ensures the horse is listening to the outside aids before starting the renvers.

# HALF-PASS

## Aids for half-pass

◆ An easy way to think of the aids is to ride a travers on a diagonal line.

◆ This keeps the forehand in front of the haunches and produces the essential elements of bend and the outside legs crossing in front of the inside ones.

◆ This half-pass position is adequate until high levels, when the horse must be shown more parallel to the track, thus demanding more bend, suppleness and balance.

Deep crossing steps show the energy and suppleness in this half-pass left.

This picture captures the crossing of the hind legs with a clear bend to the right.

## Half-pass – the young horse

◆ A young horse should already be familiar with shoulder-in and travers before starting half-pass.

### SUGGESTED EXERCISE

**a** Begin with some shoulder-in and travers steps to check that the horse is listening and on the aids.

◆ At the end of the long side, ride a demi-volte (see Glossary) and then with a diagonal line, return to the track with a few travers steps.

◆ Introducing half-pass this way should be easier for the young horse as you are only introducing one new element; namely the travers on a diagonal instead of a straight line. Keep the angle shallow to start with so that the horse can preserve his impulsion, bend and balance.

- ◆ Develop by riding more steps, such as centre line to outside track, then eventually across the whole diagonal.

- ◆ Only gradually develop a more parallel position as strength and suppleness improve.

**b** If you have difficulties, be prepared to correct back a stage; this means return to a point in the training where the horse is confident. So it may be necessary to revisit the shoulder-in or travers or simply to refresh the impulsion with some medium trot.

# PROBLEMS WITH HALF-PASS

## 1. Horse resists the leg

### CAUSE

It can be that the rider's leg aid is too strong, making the horse uncomfortable and cause him to push back against the leg or even kick out against it. If we remember that a horse is sensitive enough to feel a fly landing on his side, then clearly he can feel our leg too.

### SOLUTIONS

**a** Try using the outside leg more softly and in an on/off way. Sometimes the horse will respond better to these gentle reminders.

**b** Take care that the outside leg is not pulled too far back and with the heel scraping upwards; this can make many horses resentful. Instead ensure your leg is only one or two hand widths behind the girth and with the heel down.

**c** Of course if the preparation has not been thorough, the horse may resist the leg because he does not understand what is being asked of him. Ensure he is established in shoulder-in and travers before starting half-pass work.

### SUGGESTED EXERCISE

- ◆ Combine two exercises he should already know and spiral from a large to a small circle with slight haunches-in positioning,

- ◆ Then ride out of the small circle and make some half-pass steps, as he should now be responding better to your outside leg.

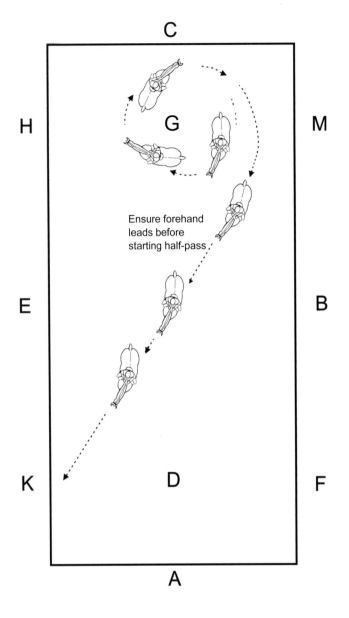

C

H

G

M

Ensure forehand
leads before
starting half-pass

E

B

K

D

F

A

Ride haunches-in on a 10m circle. This provides the necessary bend. When the horse accepts the outside leg aid and moves away from, not against it, leave the circle and with the forehand *positioned in advance of the haunches*, ask for half-pass.

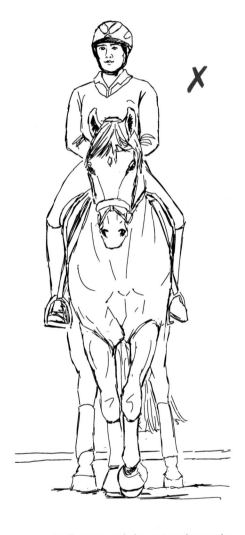

X

Compare the illustration with the previous photographs of half-passes. In both the riders have the horse clearly bending around the inside leg at the girth. In the illustration, there is no bend through the body.

# 2. Lacks bend – instead performs a leg-yield

See the illustration opposite.

## CAUSES

◆ Often caused by stiffness and loss of balance.

◆ Half-pass is more difficult than a leg-yield, because he has to move in the direction of bending, which requires greater strength and hind leg engagement, and is therefore more demanding of his balance.

◆ In leg-yield, he moves forwards and sideways with little or no bending. In effect the rider pushes the horse's weight over, which is easier for the horse, and why it is introduced at an earlier stage than the half-pass.

## SOLUTIONS: SUGGESTED EXERCISES

**a** Alternate shoulder-in and half-pass.

  ◆ Ride a few steps of shoulder-in on the track, then half-halt and, stepping down into the inside stirrup, ask for a few half-pass steps, then another half-halt, more shoulder-in parallel to the track, half-halt and more half-pass. Continue alternating between the two movements until you reach the short end of the arena.

  ◆ The addition of shoulder-in helps the horse to find the bend and to maintain it through the half-pass.

  ◆ Alternating the movements helps keep the horse focused and improves control if the horse tends to rush through the exercise.

**b** Ride travers along the wall. This supports the horse's direction of travel whilst still requiring the outside hind leg to cross, with an inside bend.

  ◆ Develop the exercise by riding a square in the middle third of the arena, riding alternate sides in travers and shoulder-in.

  ◆ This tests both the horse's obedience and the rider's co-ordination.

  ◆ It improves suppleness in the haunches and loins, enhancing bending.

**c** If the horse finds it difficult to maintain the bend all the way across the diagonal, make the exercise easier by introducing a 10m circle at X.

  ◆ Ride half-pass to the centre line at X. Then ride a small circle to consolidate the bend, followed by the rest of the long diagonal in half-pass. Once the horse can manage this comfortably, try the whole long diagonal in half-pass.

This exercise helps to improve the bend in half-pass by alternating the easier shoulder-in with the more difficult half-pass. The shoulder-in prepares the horse for the bend in the half-pass.

# 3. Too much neck bend–crooked

See illustration overleaf.

## CAUSES

Rather than being ambidextrous, most horses show some degree of one-sidedness. Therefore when riding half-pass on the soft or crooked side, it is a common fault to see more bend in the neck than through the body.

## SOLUTIONS

**a** First check you are not pulling the neck into an incorrect position. Lighten your inside hand and, for guidance, just be able to see the inside eye of your horse.

 ◆ If the outside rein has been totally given away, it may allow the horse to curl his neck to the inside. It should support the horse by maintaining a steady yet elastic contact, with both hands moved slightly in the direction of travel, bringing the outside hand to the outside of the withers and allowing the horse to feel the rein on his neck.

**b** A horse that curls to the inside will avoid engaging his inside hind leg. The remedy is to encourage the inside hind leg to step under his body and support his weight. This will help him to make proper contact with both reins. Be careful not to speed up. Just create more activity.

> A correct contact in both reins comes from a straight horse which makes equal effort with both hind legs; this is how we create an even feeling in the reins.

## SUGGESTED EXERCISES

A useful exercise for the crooked horse in half-pass is to ride some leg-yield across the diagonal, then quietly introduce inside bend to make a half-pass, then if the horse begins to curl once again, switch back to the leg-yield. The horse should be almost straight (parallel to the wall) with only a hint of outside positioning. This will help maintain balance and makes it easier to introduce the inside bend of the half-pass.

 ◆ Remember the principle that to improve a crooked horse, use exercises with the opposite bend.

 ◆ For example, my horse is crooked to the right. On the right rein, I ride renvers (with left bend), K to H then at C ride half-pass right back to F.

Half-pass in trot; too much neck bend.

below The diagram shows an exercise to improve half-pass with a horse that is crooked to the right.

The renvers asks him to bend towards his stiffer left side, thus preventing him from curling his body to the right. This helps improve his straightness, so that at H we put the horse back onto a single track, maintaining the alignment as we turn onto the centre line and providing a good platform to begin the half-pass right.

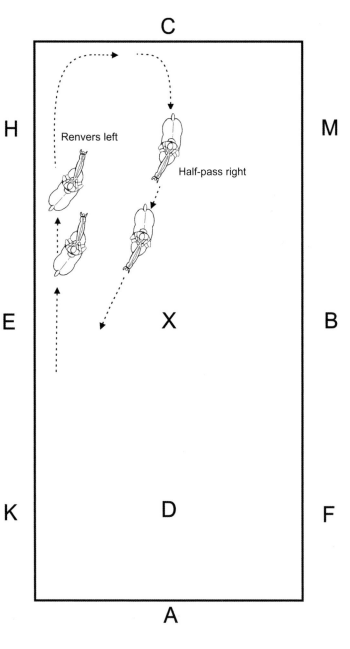

## 4. Insufficient crossing (does not apply to canter half-pass)

### CAUSES

When a walk or trot half-pass is described as 'too straight' or 'hindquarters trailing' there is normally insufficient crossing of legs.

This is usually caused by a lack of suppleness through the body or in the hind leg joints, or both.

Of course, if the rider's rein aids are too strong, this will also inhibit the horse's ability to show deep crossing steps.

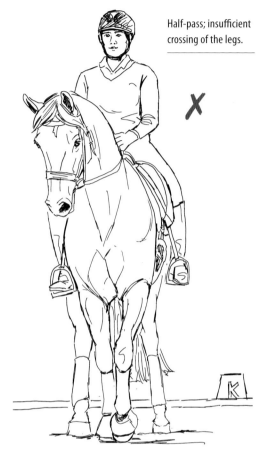

Half-pass; insufficient crossing of the legs.

### SOLUTIONS

Make sure that your horse has been thoroughly warmed up and is loose and mentally relaxed before you start. If his muscles are cold and the blood circulation is poor, do not expect him to be able to perform the exercises properly or with ease.

A young horse may not understand your aids or be strong enough to give deeply crossing steps. In the short term, lower your demands and if he can give you a few steps of a shallower half-pass, praise him. These movements take time to become fluent and we should be patient so that we do not create resistances.

### SUGGESTED EXERCISES

a  To deepen the crossing steps, try riding half-pass to half-pirouette to half-pass, all on the same rein.

  ◆  In walk, ride half-pass left, F-X-H.

  ◆  On the three-quarter line before H, half-halt and half-pirouette left, returning towards F in left half-pass.

  ◆  At the three-quarter line before F, half-halt and ride another half-pirouette left, returning towards H in left half-pass.

  ◆  Repeating this a few times on both reins helps to close up the haunches and improves the depth of the crossing steps.

  ◆  At the trot, replace the half-pirouette with a small half-circle, with haunches-in. This helps to engage the hindquarters and closes the horse from the haunches forward towards the bridle.

> **Note** – always take care to have the shoulders in advance of the haunches during the half-pass.

**b** As a training option, try asking for the full-pass (also known as full travers) in walk. From the halt the horse is moved sideways with an inside bend, but with no or only minimal forward progress. It was originally used in the cavalry to correct distances between troopers, although our emphasis is on gaining a better reaction to the sideways aid.

- For example, begin at B and aim to ride full-pass to X, and finishing at the halt. In the beginning one can allow a little forward progress. However, as there is little forward movement, it must be used sparingly, and it is recommended that having finished the full-pass steps, you ride forward boldly to refresh the horse's forward instinct.

- During the full-pass, the rider must take care to remain soft in his hands, and to ensure that his weight does not slip to the outside, which would unbalance the horse. After practising on both reins, return to the half-pass and see if it has improved the sideways steps. The goal is for the horse's legs to show a clear letter 'X' when they cross.

**c** If you have an experienced trainer with you, they may be able to help you from the ground. If they are familiar with in-hand work, a piaffe whip can be used to touch the horse softly on the outside hind leg to encourage a deeper crossing step during the half-pass. This should be done in rhythm with the rider's aids, and in such a way that the horse does not feel threatened.

> It must be stressed that safety is of paramount importance. The potential of a horse kicking out must never be forgotten and this work should only be practiced by an experienced person, who has familiarised the horse with in-hand techniques so that he is not frightened of the whip. It must not be used carelessly or roughly, but with tact and softly. The trainer must always watch the *whole* horse when working close to him and be aware of danger signs and be ready to cease the action of the whip and step quietly away.
>
> **If in doubt, do not do it!**

# 5. Hindquarters leading

## CAUSES

Is often due to insufficient impulsion or incorrect positioning, or if the rider is too strong with the outside leg aid.

## SOLUTIONS

**a** Take care to maintain activity in the haunches with your inside leg before and during the half-pass.

In effect, we have to strike a balance between the forward movement and the sideways element. When riders first begin two-track work, it is a common fault to focus too much on the sideways steps. We should remember that the point of lateral work is to improve the gymnastic qualities of our horse and that means *both* forwards and sideways steps.

## SUGGESTED EXERCISE

◆ To improve impulsion, ride the first half of the long diagonal to X in medium trot, then collect and from X, ride half-pass the rest of the long diagonal.

◆ When using this exercise, it can be helpful to think of riding the half-pass after X as a travers on a diagonal line, with the rider maintaining the forehand exactly on the line of the long diagonal and the haunches moved to the inside in a bend around the inside leg.

Half-pass, hindquarters leading.

◆ The rider should line up the destination marker between the horse's ears, and not allow any deviation from this point. This will improve accuracy and help with correct positioning.

**b** A rider may cause the hindquarters to lead by using the outside leg too strongly behind the girth. Do not clamp the outside leg on to the horse; try using intermittent touches from your leg. This is particularly so if the horse is very sensitive.

◆ When we communicate with each other, we have a range of tones to use in our voice; and when we ride, we should also have a range of communication. Sometimes the horse will listen better to a 'whispering' aid.

◆ The aim is that we train our horses to respond to light, almost invisible aids, which is better for both horse and rider and looks more elegant. The rider should not be working harder than the horse!

c The contact in the outside rein may be too strong. This will slow down the forehand in the half-pass, so that the hindquarters overtake. The answer is to reduce the outside rein contact and allow both reins to operate in the direction of the half-pass to allow proper positioning of the shoulders slightly in advance of the haunches.

## 6. Horse runs sideways/anticipates half-pass

### CAUSES

It can happen that the horse slides to the side either as an evasion or because he anticipates what you are about to ask him.

Half-pass, trot;
head tilting.

### SOLUTIONS: SUGGESTED EXERCISES

Start half-pass from the beginning of the long side, then after a few steps half-halt and ride straight forward, parallel to the wall for a few metres then resume half-pass either in the same direction, or to the other hand.

◆ Alternatively, interrupt the half-pass with transitions or a circle. The point is to stop the horse from guessing what we want and encourage him to listen to our aids.

## 7. Head tilting

### CAUSES

When the muzzle tilts it is a fault as there will be uneven contact and this can become a problem if the horse learns to lock his poll as an evasion. Often the cause is too strong a rein contact on one side. It is important to address this issue at the earliest opportunity.

For example, if the horse's right ear dips lower and the muzzle lifts up to the left, it indicates that the left hand is too strong.

## SOLUTIONS

◆ It can happen that the rider tries to bend the horse in the half-pass too much with the reins alone, leading to discomfort and a head tilt.

◆ The answer is to create a uniform bend through the body with both legs; the inside leg at the girth also asks for impulsion whilst the outside leg behind the girth prevents the haunches escaping the bend to the outside.

◆ The rider should also lighten the rein on the side to which the muzzle tilts (muzzle lifts on left side, lighten left rein; muzzle lifts on right side, lighten right rein).

# CANTER HALF-PASS

Many problems are common to half-pass in walk, trot and canter, but there are some specific differences which need consideration.

One obvious difference is that the horse's legs do not cross in canter half-pass. Instead the horse 'bounds' sideways during the moment of suspension, maintaining his bend, balance and suppleness. See photo overleaf.

# PROBLEMS WITH CANTER HALF-PASS

## 1. Too little sideways movement

### SOLUTIONS

**a** Be sure the canter is in balance. It will be very difficult to ride canter half-pass if the stride is long, flat and rapid. The quality of the collected canter is a big factor in producing a good half-pass.

The more he can engage the haunches, that is, tuck his pelvis and step well under his body to carry weight on them, the better will be his balance and he will able be to show a better half-pass.

If the haunches are weak, he will struggle to show the half-pass. We must work to build him, otherwise he will be leaning on his shoulders and heavy in the reins.

We can test for self-carriage by giving one rein then both; the horse should remain in balance and not fall onto his shoulder. If he does, then we need to improve the canter before attempting the half-pass.

The canter should have plenty of 'jump' in the hind legs without becoming faster. Activity does not mean more speed.

Unlike walk or trot, in canter half-pass the legs do not cross.

## SUGGESTED EXERCISES

◆ To improve the horse's reaction to the leg aids for the canter half-pass, ride a square in the middle third of the arena, alternating one side shoulder-fore then the next in travers and so on.

This is also an excellent exercise in its own right for suppling the horse in the area behind the saddle, but should only be ridden *if your trainer is sure that you can straighten your horse after the travers, otherwise it may be counterproductive.*

- We can improve the carrying capacity of the hindquarters by riding many transitions within the canter. For example on a large circle ride half the circle in working canter and the second half in collection; or perhaps from collected to medium and back again.

- Alternatively, ride a diamond pattern in the arena. On the right rein, from B ride a diagonal line in collected canter, then at A turn and ride working or medium strides, at E turn and ride collected canter again towards C and so on.

Square exercise in canter. This exercise is very good to improve obedience to our aids, besides developing suppleness and engagement. Be sure to keep the sides of the square straight

Diamond exercise in canter. This pattern uses different lines in the arena and requires the rider to properly balance the horse with halfhalts before turning to make the transition. This can enhance the quality of the gait.

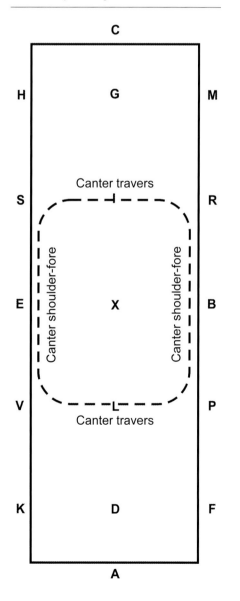

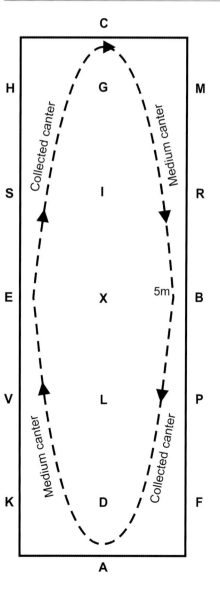

**b** The timing of the sideways aids is important. The time to apply the outside leg is as the withers rise in the canter sequence. In this moment of suspension all four legs are briefly off the ground and so the horse is then able to bound sideways. He cannot do this when the hooves are on the ground.

**c** If the horse resists the half-pass aids, improve his responses by holding the schooling whip on the horse's side by the outside leg as you apply the aid. Note that the whip is just pressed against the horse.

**e** If the horse is trying to respond to the correct half-pass aids but the results are still not enough, then it is likely that the horse is not yet supple enough and further work will be needed to increase the scope and reach of the lateral strides.

### SUGGESTED EXERCISE

Starting at the track, ride just two or three strides of half-pass and then rebalance with a few strides of shoulder-fore parallel to the track. Then some more half-pass and further shoulder-fore. Breaking the movement down into smaller more manageable sections can make the exercise easier for the horse and allows the rider to make corrections to the balance when necessary.

## ZIG-ZAG IN HALF-PASS

The zig-zag is normally performed either side of the centre line and is a good test of the horse's inside hind leg engagement on each rein. In trot, the distance covered in either direction is measured in metres, whereas in canter we ask for a specific number of strides to either hand.

## PROBLEMS WITH ZIG-ZAG IN HALF-PASS

### 1. Crookedness

A common problem is a loss of straightness; the haunches can overtake the fore-hand after the change which leaves the horse crooked after each change of hand.

### SOLUTIONS

**a** It is a mistake to continue the exercise when the horse is crooked, as it can become an evasion to collection. If the fault persists, stop the zig-zag and ride the horse forward with energy. Try using circles of increasing and decreasing size. Riding shoulder-in is also helpful to correct the quarters from leading.

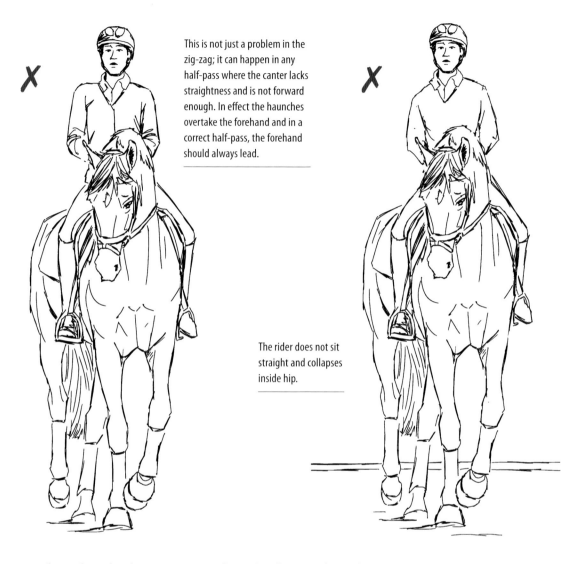

This is not just a problem in the zig-zag; it can happen in any half-pass where the canter lacks straightness and is not forward enough. In effect the haunches overtake the forehand and in a correct half-pass, the forehand should always lead.

The rider does not sit straight and collapses inside hip.

**b** Perhaps the rider does not sit straight and collapses a hip. This can unbalance the horse and throw him out of alignment.

Think of stretching the inside leg down (without it pushing forwards) and at the same time, lift the inside collarbone up and a little back, so that the shoulders are not only parallel to the ground, but also parallel to the horse's shoulders too. This should straighten the rider's posture in the saddle and enable him to remain in balance with the horse.

**c** The rider should remember to straighten the horse before moving into the next segment of the zig-zag.

◆ The rider's inside leg should maintain the forward activity to keep the straightness, and with soft half-halts, bring the forehand into a shoulder-fore position, (changing his seat, leg and rein positioning to the new bend as he does so) then bends the horse in the new direction and rides forwards and sideways.

◆ This phase of 'old half-pass-straighten – new half-pass' can take two canter strides to accomplish. (In trot, it can take up to three steps.)

◆ When a rider is first learning the zig-zag, he may not be able to achieve this essential straightening in only two canter strides; no problem, take one or two more strides to allow time to set up the horse properly. Also, ride fewer strides in each direction, otherwise you may run out of room in the arena!

◆ As straightening becomes more instinctive for the rider, he can progress by taking fewer strides. This way the rider can learn to co-ordinate his aiding and the horse does not get confused or slip into bad habits.

d Crookedness can be caused by an anxious rider moving his body too much during the change of direction, and this can be enough to throw the horse off balance, resulting in swinging and the quarters leading.

*... sit very still and concentrate on the feel of the horse underneath you.*

◆ The answer is to sit very still and concentrate on the feel of the horse underneath you. This should help you improve the timing and co-ordination of your aiding.

◆ If the exercise demands many changes of hand and steep half-passes, try making it easier with less acute angles and fewer changes of hand until you can achieve smooth transfers in either direction.

## 2. Problems with the flying change in the zig-zag

a If the rider can show correctly positioned half-passes in either direction, then it points us towards considering the moment of flying change.

◆ Whilst maintaining the bend in the old direction, ensure that the last strides of half-pass before the change are as parallel to the track as possible; this will make the beginning of half-pass in the new direction much easier to control.

◆ Think of preparing the flying change by bending the horse in the new direction before asking for the change of lead.

b The more steps demanded in either direction, the more difficult is the movement as the angle of half-pass is steeper. If the haunches are trailing, try making the exercise easier by having fewer steps in each direction. Then, as the horse's confidence and balance improves, one can gradually ask for more.

c Sometimes the rider has difficulty in making the horse straight at the beginning of the zig-zag.

◆ To help, try starting the exercise on the track. The wall will help the rider check for straightness. Then half-pass in a few strides only, straighten, ride the flying change parallel to the wall and return to the wall, straighten and change again. When this feels secure, progress to riding the zig-zag either side of the centre line.

## 3. Rider loses accuracy

SOLUTIONS

a Take care to count the number of strides you are riding. Ensure you are aware of how many you have ridden.

◆ Remember that the flying change is the first stride of the half-pass in the new direction. For example, if you are on the centre line and are performing three strides right, six strides left, then three right, then count 'one, two, three, change, two, three, four, five six, change, two, three, straight'. This should bring you back onto the centre line.

b If you have trouble keeping your lines accurate, look ahead through your horse's ears, pick a reference point in the arena to aim at, and keep your eyes fixed on it. Then you will need to choose another point for the change of hand in the zig-zag. If you can keep your focus on your chosen points, it will improve your accuracy.

## 4. My horse does not change in time

SOLUTION

This problem is essentially one of reaction to the aids. Go back and ensure single flying changes are absolutely reliable when you ask for them. If they are not, then your horse is not ready for the zig-zag.

## 5. Changes are early/anticipates the change

SOLUTION

a If the horse changes early, it can be that he is tense, so take time to relax him and make sure you are not the cause of his tension by asking too strongly for the change.

during the pirouette. This requires feel and timing from the rider and if you find this difficult, ask your trainer to call when you should apply each leg. The aid should be given in the moment just as the relevant hind hoof is about to leave the ground. (So inside leg controls inside hind leg and rider's outside leg controls the outside hind.)

**b** As mentioned above, the pirouette may be too small and cause the horse to lose his rhythm. If increasing the drive from the inside leg does not solve the problem, make the movement larger.

**c** The inside hind leg should pick up and put down in the rhythm of the pace. Sometimes one sees that it sticks on the ground for one or more steps.

- ◆ This can be due to excessive rein action, which stifles the impulsion. The rider should make small yields within the rein contact to allow the horse to flow. He must be able to move forwards a tiny amount as well as sideways.

## 3. Falls onto inside shoulder

A correctly ridden pirouette requires suppleness, balance and engagement. If these are lacking, then it may happen that the horse falls to the inside.

### SOLUTIONS

**a** Too much inside rein can cause the horse to lean against the hand and therefore when he turns his weight is on the forehand and falls to the inside. The rider should not be tempted to pull the horse with the inside rein into the pirouette. As in any circle, it is a combination of seat, leg and rein aids. The pirouette is a very small two-track circle, so the effect of any faulty aiding tends to be magnified.

The inside rein should guide the horse's direction in coordination with the other aids. It should never be the dominant aid.

**b** A lack of hind leg activity can also leave the horse on his forehand with the result that he falls to the inside. Improve your forward driving from the inside leg or if the horse feels lazy, perhaps ride some energetic canter, then a transition to collected walk and start the pirouette as soon as possible. The canter may energise the walk and help maintain impulsion.

**c** Lateral stiffness may be the problem. If the horse is stiff, he may lose balance when you attempt the pirouette and fall to the inside.

Try establishing the bend in shoulder-in, and then half-halt and ride a quarter-pirouette. The less demanding shoulder-in can then be seen as preparing the horse for the requirements of the pirouette.

If this does not help, you may need to consider postponing the pirouette until more suppling work is done. When the horse is established in shoulder-in, travers and renvers, he ought to be capable of the pirouette too – providing we are asking him properly.

**d** Either through lack of balance in the turn, or from anticipation, the horse may 'spin' rather step rhythmically.

◆ You can deal with this by riding only one or two steps of pirouette, then ride out of it with a straight horse. Breaking the movement up into smaller segments can give you more control of what happens beneath you.

◆ Turning your shoulders more slowly during the pirouette can also help.

## 4. Hind legs move to the inside rather than stepping under the weight

The hind legs should neither cross nor move to the inside; instead they should describe a tiny circle.

*The hind legs should neither cross nor move to the inside; instead they should describe a tiny circle.*

### SOLUTIONS

The problem can be too much outside leg. In trying to prevent the haunches escaping to the outside, the rider can over-compensate and push the haunches inwards by mistake. Make the aid much lighter.

◆ If the horse is very sensitive, take the outside leg behind the girth as usual, but barely, if at all, touch his side with it. Taking the leg back will place the rider's weight aid correctly onto the inside seat bone. Although the horse will be aware of your leg, if it remains very light he should accept it rather than move away from it.

◆ Begin the pirouette from a shoulder-in. Bringing the forehand to the inside is a good preparation and makes it less likely that the haunches will move to the inside.

◆ If the walk is active prior to the pirouette, then with half-halts we can enhance engagement, making the forehand lighter. This will make it easier to turn, and so the rider can use lighter, more sophisticated aids, reducing the need for a strong outside leg.

# CANTER PIROUETTE

## General

◆ This is a small circle on two tracks, with the forehand moving around the quarters.

◆ It is important that the three-beat rhythm is maintained throughout.

◆ There should be a noticeable lowering of the haunches as the horse carries more weight on the hind legs, thus lightening the forehand, making it possible to perform the pirouette.

◆ The movement can be ridden as a full, half or quarter pirouette.

A full canter pirouette to the right, clearly showing the horse's strength as he takes weight back onto his haunches. Only by sitting in this way can the horse lighten the forehand enough to make the small 360° turn and keep the canter rhythm.

- The number of strides taken can vary, but on average expect six to eight in a full pirouette and three to four in a half.

## Aids for canter pirouette

- Prepare the horse by asking for increased collection and cadence in the canter. This should feel as though the canter is more 'on the spot' but never losing its jump or elasticity.

- Sometimes referred to as the 'pirouette canter', the rider seeks to encourage greater bending of the hind leg at the hocks. This requires strength from the horse as extra weight is carried by the inside hind leg. The poll should remain the highest point.

- The inside leg aids at the girth to maintain impulsion and is the leg around which the horse bends his body.

- The outside leg a little behind the girth asks for the pirouette and prevents the haunches from escaping to the outside.

- The inside rein shows the flexion and the sideways movement required.

- The outside rein helps to control the rhythm and also the amount of bend and flexion.

- When the pirouette is finished, the rider should be positive in riding out of the movement; use the inside leg at the girth and the outside rein to guide the horse on to a straight line.

# PROBLEMS WITH CANTER PIROUETTE

## 1. The pirouette is too large

This might indicate that the canter lacked sufficient collection and that the strides were too long and not seated.

> The essence of collection is how much weight the horse can take back and carry on his haunches.
>
> Shorter strides are not the main aim in collection; they should be the result of increased engagement of the hind legs.

This demonstrates the extra collection required for the pirouette. Notice the pronounced bending of the hind legs and the lowering of the croup.

## SOLUTIONS

There are a number of exercises to develop collection.

### SUGGESTED EXERCISES

◆ Cantering circles of decreasing size is a good starting point, but be certain to preserve the bend, balance and 'jump' in the strides. If activity is lost, refresh the energy by riding some medium strides on a large circle or straight line.

◆ Cantering in a slight travers position – about two hooves width is sufficient – on a straight line is good for developing suppleness. When ridden on a spiral, we can approach a pirouette with good bend, but be sure to straighten the horse just before starting the pirouette itself.

◆ If the horse is capable of a pirouette, but it is too big, we can use the arena wall to help. Ride counter-canter along the three-quarter line. Near the end of the long side develop the 'pirouette canter' and ask the horse to make a half-pirouette towards the wall, and then continue along the three-quarter line in true canter. The presence of the wall helps to prevent the horse from moving forwards too much. As the horse improves, the rider can begin with a line that is a little closer to the wall to make smaller pirouettes.

The rider may be asking too much too soon from the horse. It is logical to be able to ride good, seated quarter then half pirouettes before attempting the full version.

♦ Ride a square with slight travers position. As you approach each corner, prepare by straightening and asking for the maximum collection your horse is capable of, before asking for a quarter pirouette. Ride positively forward after each turn so your horse does not drift sideways. The square should have straight sides.

♦ When this exercise is secure, make the square smaller so that the corners come more quickly; this is good preparation for the rider to think and act promptly. Then the horse should be ready to try the half pirouette.

♦ For half pirouettes, ride a three-loop serpentine. On reaching the centre line, ride a half pirouette, then continue on the same lead to the next loop and repeat, starting and finishing the exercise on the same rein. Executing the half pirouette on the centre line provides a useful visual measure for the rider to gauge the size of the pirouette.

If the rider is not using his seat correctly, the horse cannot be brought sufficiently onto his haunches for the pirouette. The horse would have no chance of making a small pirouette and must not be blamed for a mistake that is not his.

♦ As noted above, we cannot collect our horse by pulling on his mouth. It takes time and a skilful combination of seat, legs and reins to produce an athletic horse, strong enough to carry more weight on his haunches. (See chapter on 'The Seat' for details.)

A lack of suppleness can be the problem. Using lateral exercises can help.

♦ For example, ride canter half-pass from the track to the centre line at D or G.

♦ Then ride a small half-circle in travers, straighten, then ride more canter half-pass. This combination of movements helps to close the horse from the haunches. As the horse progresses, ride a half pirouette at the end of the half-pass instead. One should notice an improvement in both movements.

## 2. Hind legs hop together

A correct pirouette maintains the leg sequence of canter. Loss of impulsion can be the cause of the hind legs both stepping at the same time.

### SOLUTIONS

**a** Keep a light rein contact as you approach the pirouette; if it is too strong it can smother the horse's ability to go forward with energy.

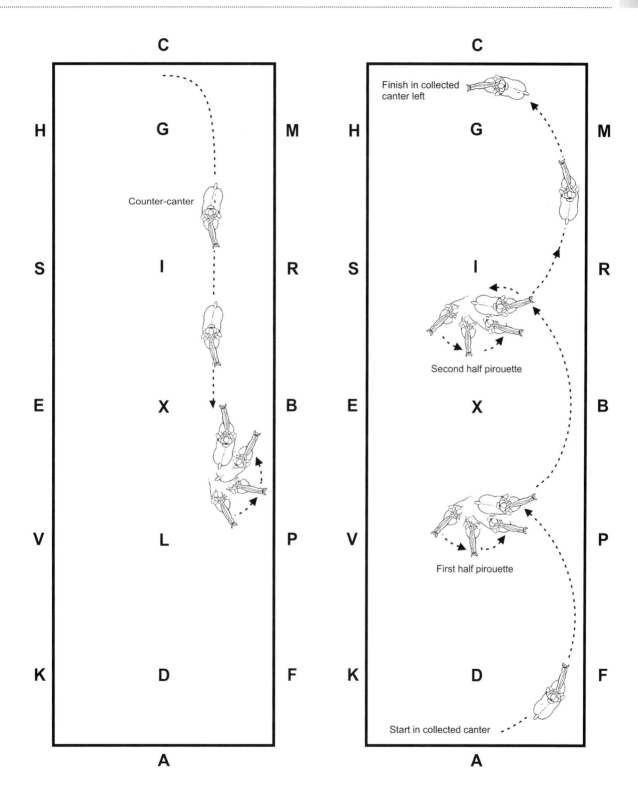

C

H     G     M

Counter-canter

S     I     R

E     X     B

V     L     P

K     D     F

A

C

Finish in collected canter left

H     G     M

S     I     R

Second half pirouette

E     X     B

V     P

First half pirouette

K     D     F

Start in collected canter

A

141

**b** Ride medium canter, next collect towards the 'pirouette canter' then ride the movement. If the horse begins the movement correctly but 'bunny hops' part way through, ride fewer pirouette steps followed by medium canter to keep him thinking forwards.

However it may be that he is not quite strong enough to perform the full pirouette and needs more time to develop his strength.

## 3. Quarters fall out

A horse may try to evade carrying weight on his inside hind leg by pushing the quarters out.

### SOLUTIONS

**a** Be sure that the outside leg is in position behind the girth to prevent the haunches escaping. If the horse persists, use the leg a little stronger in rhythm with the strides.

**b** School your horse in the travers, and ensure that you can switch from straight to the lateral strides at will. This can improve obedience to the outside leg aid. Again a square can be ridden, with alternating sides of travers, then straight or even shoulder-fore.

**c** The pirouette is a taxing movement for the horse, requiring considerable strength and balance. If the rider practises it too long and often, there is a danger of straining the hind legs.

### SUGGESTED EXERCISE

*Stiffness in the rider will produce a stiff horse …*

◆ In training, use the less demanding 'working pirouette', where the hind legs are allowed to move on a circle of about 2m diameter. This still allows the rider to practise the aids whilst keeping the bend and rhythm.

**d** For a good pirouette, the rider must be still and supple. Stiffness in the rider will produce a stiff horse, and should the rider collapse his inside hip, then his seat and weight will be likely to slip to the outside, upsetting the horse's balance and leading to the quarters escaping. A faulty seat will produce faulty movements!

## 4. Falling on to inside shoulder

This can demonstrate a lack of suppleness or a fault in the rider's seat.

### SOLUTIONS

**a** Ensure that the horse is responding to the inside leg aid.

- Ride shoulder-fore to check that he is not leaning on the inside rein. We should be able to connect the horse to the outside rein with our inside leg, not by pulling the outside rein harder.

- In canter there should be a very slight bend around the rider's inside leg, created by our inside body positioning (see chapter on 'The Seat'). If he is not supple enough to do this, he is not ready to be trained for the pirouette.

**b** Anticipation by the horse can be a problem and he may turn too quickly and lose balance.

- Think of turning your own shoulders more slowly so that he copies your body movement. Make sure you take the initiative so that he reacts to you and not the other way around.

**c** A crooked horse will be out of balance and may fall onto his shoulder when attempting to pirouette.

- In this case spend time on straightening the horse. Riding counter-canter and moving between travers, shoulder-fore and straightness are all very helpful.

> *A faulty seat will produce faulty movements!*

## 5. Heavy on the forehand

If the horse is on his shoulder, the pirouette will appear laboured. The forehand should appear to rise during the turning steps, as result of the haunches lowering.

### SOLUTIONS

If the horse is not through in his back, a poor pirouette is the only expectation. The poll should remain the highest point and the weight should shift from the forehand to the haunches.

- Try and prepare the canter better with frequent transitions both between the gaits and within them. Maintaining a round elastic topline is important and the rider can give and take the reins occasionally to test for self carriage.

- Periodically ride a few strides of 'extreme' collection and again test for self carriage. The horse cannot be light if the rider is strong in his hands.

- Seek to produce the collection with the lightest rein contact, whilst preserving the essential elements of the horse connected to the bit by the forward pushing aids, (not pulling hands) with an elastic topline and engaged haunches.

CHAPTER

# 6

# MORE ADVANCED CANTER WORK

## COUNTER-CANTER

Counter-canter was introduced in Chapter 4; now we can explore it further.

### General

- ◆ It strengthens the haunches, as it requires straightness and therefore even load-carrying by each hind leg. It straightens and supples the horse.

- ◆ The tempo should remain regular and unhurried.

- ◆ Most young horses find it a difficult exercise, unless they have a naturally very well-balanced canter, so introduce with tact.

- ◆ The ease with which the horse performs the counter-canter can be a good measure of his readiness to start flying changes.

### Introducing counter-canter

It is advisable to teach the counter-canter from walk.

#### SUGGESTED EXERCISES

1 A simple way is to begin by riding shallow loops (single serpentines), 3 to 5m deep on the long side of the arena.

- ◆ From the corner marker, smoothly bring the horse away from the track. When he is level with the half marker (B or E) quietly return to the last corner marker, so your horse is straight with all four hooves on the track as your shoulder passes the letter.

◆ The second half of the loop is the counter-canter part, so this is a gentle way to introduce the exercise.

◆ Throughout the loop, maintain the inside positioning of your seat, legs and reins.

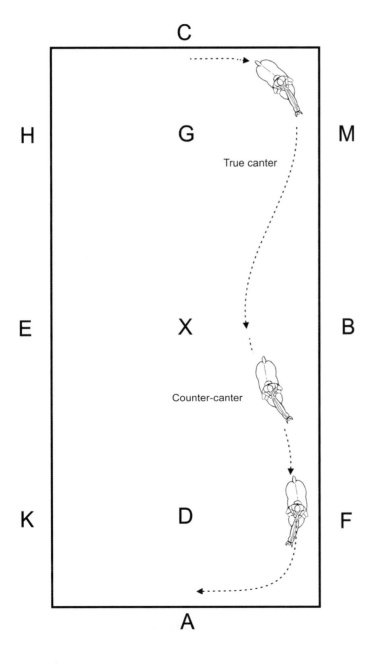

The diagrams, here, and on the following pages suggest methods of developing counter-canter. A shallow loop (single serpentine) of 3 to 5m deep is the easiest way to introduce the movement.

The half 15m circle and short diagonal approach are more demanding of balance as the angle of return to the track increases.

Riding walk half-pass into counter-canter is more sophisticated and should ensure that balance and engagement are established before starting the counter-canter.

- Ride the second half of the loop tactfully by guiding him with your inside leg at the girth. Make it easier by looking at the point you want to ride to.

- When your horse can show loops 3 to 5m deep comfortably, gradually make them more pronounced by riding towards X – creating a 10m deep loop.

2 The next stage could be to make half a 15m circle at the end of the long side, then return to the track between the half and corner markers, so that there are a few counter-canter strides on the outside track.

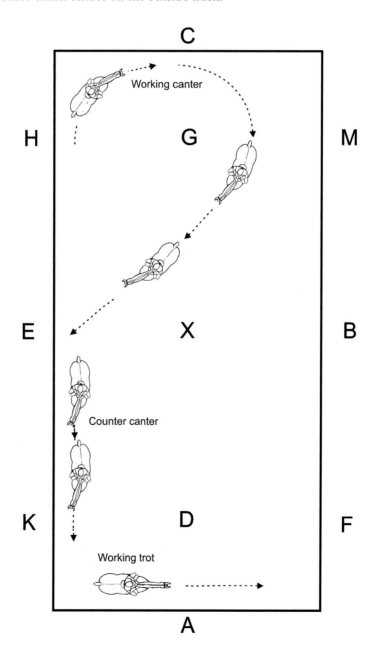

3 Alternatively, ride across the short diagonal to change rein, then make some counter-canter strides on the opposite track. If your horse has problems maintaining counter-canter, correct back a stage and ride some easier shallow loops again.

4 Another option is to ride walk half-pass from A or C to the half markers, E or B. When you arrive at the track, ask for the counter-canter, using the half-pass bend as the preparation. Walk just before the first corner.

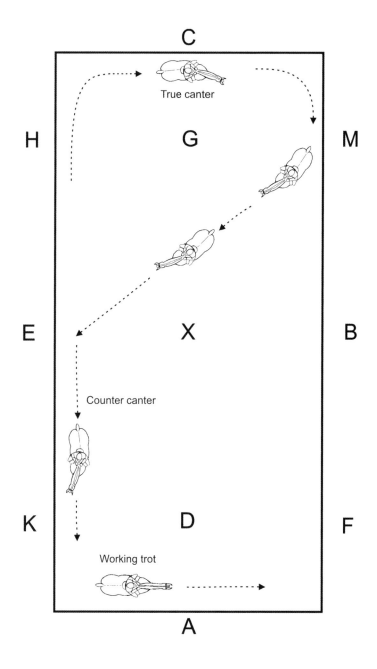

## SOLUTIONS

- Review your preparation; give your horse a chance by using half-halts to ask him to sit a little more, whilst keeping an even rhythm, before starting the exercise.

- Be sure to stay seated in the saddle; tipping forwards will speed him up.

- Be prepared to offer small forward yields of the reins to encourage the horse to stay relaxed. Taking a stronger hold of his mouth will make him pull back on you.

## 3. Carries haunches to one side

One of the principle aims of counter-canter is to straighten (align) the horse. So it is important that we do not let the horse swing his haunches to counter-canter on two tracks instead of one.

## SOLUTIONS

*We should always correct crookedness by aligning the forehand with the haunches.*

If the horse begins the canter incorrectly by bringing his haunches to the inside, the rider should ask for a shoulder-fore position before giving the canter aid. We should always correct crookedness by aligning the forehand with the haunches.

- Keep the outside leg behind the girth light. If it is too strong, the horse may interpret this as a lateral aid and obey your faulty instruction!

- Do not bend the horse's neck too much towards the leading leg. This can cause him to curl his haunches in and lean his weight onto the outside shoulder. Think of an almost straight horse in counter-canter, with just a slight bend around your inside leg at the girth.

- Ride the counter-canter with balanced but bounding strides. It is easier to maintain a straight horse if there is some positive energy to channel, but do not over-ride and push him onto his shoulder, for then he will stiffen.

## 4. Stiffens

This can be because the exercise is too demanding, or because the rider stiffens his body.

## SOLUTIONS

If the exercise is beyond the horse's current level of suppleness, he may brace his body in an effort to keep balance. In this situation, try making a simpler counter-canter pattern. We should always be sensitive to our horses and be prepared to give them more time rather than force the issue.

- A rider who stiffens his body will have the same effect on his horse. As noted above, he must sit quietly and avoid twisting his body or becoming rigid. When he can ride with quiet harmony, he will be an asset, not a hindrance, to his horse.

# SIMPLE CHANGES

See the sequence of photos overleaf.

- This is a change of canter lead through three or four walk steps – roughly one horse's length.

- Well-established simple changes are a necessary part of the preparation for flying changes.

- During the walk phase, straighten the horse (get rid of the old bend) then bend him in the new direction. Then he is ready for the new canter lead.

## SUGGESTED EXERCISES

1 We can canter across a short diagonal, walk just before the corner and in the turn, and ask for the new inside lead. The arc of the turn will help us to pick up the new lead.

2 Or canter a half 10m circle from B or E and as we approach the centre line, walk two steps, then after X two more steps with the new bend, then ask for canter. The bend of the half-circles will promote the correct strike-off, and the balance required for the half-circles will help us achieve good canter to walk transitions.

- Our aim should be that we are able to make secure simple changes on a straight line, implying that the horse and rider have become sophisticated enough to need only a slight change of bend in order to be sure of picking up the new lead.

# PROBLEMS WITH SIMPLE CHANGES

## 1. Horse does not pick up the new lead

This may reflect a lack of suppleness to one side, or poor rider preparation.

1. The picture shows the rider in right-lead canter, preparing the horse for the walk transition. We can see her outside leg correctly positioned behind the girth.

2. In this picture, the rider is in walk, but has changed her seat, leg and rein position ready for the left-lead canter departure.

3. This photo captures the moment of departure into left-lead canter. Note the 'uphill' stance of the horse as he flexes the hind leg joints to lift himself.

## SOLUTIONS

◆ Chose an exercise that helps the horse to find the new lead. Using a figure-of-eight pattern encourages the horse towards the new lead.

◆ Be precise in your aiding. The horse needs to feel the difference between your left and right canter aids.

◆ Keep your upper body still during the simple change. Rocking or twisting in the saddle can cause a mistake.

## 2. Horse trots through the change

The horse should perform three or four walk steps between canter leads; it is not a simple change if he trots.

### SOLUTIONS

◆ Preparing the canter to walk transition is important. See chapter on 'The Seat' regarding downward transitions. If this preparation is neglected, the horse may fall on to his forehand and trot instead.

See photo opposite.

*below* For a successful simple change, the canter must be prepared before the transition. Note the lowered haunches as the horse takes weight back, allowing a clean, balanced canter to walk.

- If the rider pushes with his pelvis during the downward transition, then it is difficult for the horse to walk cleanly.

- An enthusiastic horse can anticipate the simple change and trots rather than walks. Try riding just downward transitions to walk, but no canter afterwards, until he calms down and listens to the aids.

- Make the simple changes in different parts of the arena to lessen anticipation.

- If the horse is becoming strong, ride canter, walk, halt then calmly rein-back before asking for the new canter lead. See 'rein-back' on page 155.

- Asking for the canter/walk transition close to the arena wall can help if the horse is strong.

## 3. Horse loses straightness

During the simple change, the hind legs should follow the path of the forelegs.

### SOLUTIONS

- Check that you are applying your aids tactfully. Being stronger with one leg or rein can be enough to cause lack of straightness.

- Collapsing a hip will push the rider's weight to one side and produce loss of straightness. It is important to keep the correct posture at all times because it is functional, not just elegant.

- It can help to ride the simple change between two poles on the ground.

- For example, ride a 10m figure-of-eight, with the simple change over X. Place two poles parallel to each other and about 1m apart either side of the centre line at X. Riding the walk phase between the poles will help to keep your horse from swinging.

## 4. Horse is above the bit in transition

For the simple change to be correct, the horse should of course remain on the aids and show clear walk steps.

A likely cause of this problem is that the rider does not have the horse on his seat aid, and the canter is out of balance. Then, in attempting to make a walk transition, the rider pulls with his hands and the horse goes above the bit.

## SOLUTIONS

Preparing the canter is important. The aim is for a degree of self-carriage, so that the rider does not try to keep his horse on the bit with his hands. The seat must be effective and this requires correct posture.

- Riding canter to walk on straight lines is more difficult, so practise on circles and it is useful to make give and re-takes of one and then both reins to test for self carriage and to ensure that the rider is not holding a strong contact.

- A balanced canter should have the feeling of travelling up a hill at a steady speed and hind legs under his body. This will make the transition to walk easier.

- Imagine how you would make the transition if you had no reins in your hands; then you would have to use the seat aids. Try to carry this feeling with you when you make canter to walk.

*The seat must be effective and this requires correct posture.*

# REIN-BACK

- The horse moves backwards in a straight line with the legs moving in diagonal or almost diagonal pairs.

- Unlike trot, there is no moment of suspension.

- The steps should be regular and unhurried.

- He should not drag his hooves.

- The horse should remain on the bit, lift his back and show some tucking of his pelvis as he reins back.

- This will aid engagement as the hind leg joints need to flex more.

- It demonstrates throughness.

- It is quite taxing on the hind legs, so should be used in moderation.

## Riding rein-back

- Bring the horse to a square halt, remaining quietly on the aids.

- Move both legs equally back a little.

- The rider can lighten his seat a little, as if to invite the horse to lift his back, but avoid leaning well forwards. It should be almost an invisible movement.

- As the legs ask gently, the hands close softly around the reins to prevent the forwards option. When the horse offers to step back instead, the fingers soften to show approval. Repeat for each step.

- When introducing rein-back, be happy with one step back. As the horse understands, then you can build to three or four steps, approximately one horse's length.

- To finish the rein-back, move both legs forwards to the normal position then ask him to move straight ahead calmly.

- There should not be a halt before moving forwards.

## PROBLEMS WITH REIN-BACK

### 1. The horse does not stay straight

Moving crookedly to one side is a fault. There may be a number of causes.

### SOLUTIONS

**a** Try making the rein-back on the track, so that the wall helps to keep your horse straight.

- If he still deviates inwards, try the rein-back between two poles on the ground. He will want to avoid stepping on either pole and this can help you.

**b** Be sure that you are sitting evenly in the saddle and not unbalancing him. It is important to be even with the aids. If one rein or leg is stronger than the opposite side, this can cause crookedness.

**c** It may be caused by the horse trying to avoid engaging one hind leg. For example, if he steps to the left, then apply your left leg a little more than the right or move it slightly further back.

*Note that this is not contradicting the normal rule of applying the aids evenly; it is a correction for a specific situation.*

**d** Ensure that the halt preceding the rein-back is straight and square. Without this, the horse will find it almost impossible to rein-back properly.

## 2. Horse resists/does not step back

◆ Some horses are nervous of stepping backwards. Although they have almost all-round vision, there is a blind spot immediately behind their hindquarters and that is where we are asking them to step. They need to trust that there is no danger there.

◆ Others do not understand what we are asking for.

◆ For some horses, not stepping back is a sign of disobedience.

### SOLUTIONS

**a** In many cases the best option is to teach rein-back from the ground. This can be done with young horses as a lesson in trust and to check that the horse respects the wishes of the handler, by moving back when asked. This can be taught in the stable, so that the horse learns good manners and does not barge into the human space.

◆ With the horse wearing a cavesson, the handler asks the horse to take a step back with soft half-halts on the lunge line. If he does not move, then place a hand on his chest and squeeze a little, and use your voice. As soon as he steps back, stop and praise him. Repeat a few times until the horse understands easily.

◆ When he is responding positively in the stable, we can try in the arena. Bring the horse to a square halt beside the wall to keep him straight. Then repeat what you did in the stable, so that you have only changed one thing – the place where you are doing the exercise.

◆ If he does not listen to the half-halts, do not become rough with them, otherwise he will lose his sensitivity and you will make problems for the future. Instead, touch him alternately on the fetlocks with a schooling whip as you give your voice aid, to give him the idea of moving back in diagonal pairs.

◆ Be patient; losing your temper will make the situation worse. Reward any step back he makes and show that you are pleased with him.

◆ Establish the rein-back at the same place in the arena so he knows what to expect, but as soon as he understands, try it at other points around the arena.

◆ If he resists when under saddle, be careful not to pull harder on the reins. Some horses will rear if they feel this, or they rein-back with a hollow back, dragging their hooves.

> *Reward any step back he makes and show that you are pleased with him.*

♦ If he does not respond, your trainer can help from the ground, either by squeezing the horse's chest gently as you give the aids, or touching the fetlocks alternately with the whip. As always, patience is needed to teach him correctly.

**b** Check that your hands have not become hard and un-yielding. There is no profit in having a trial of strength with your horse. Riding is about technique and feel, not brutality! Ask with soft squeezes and remember to reduce the aid the moment he offers to step back. Show him that he earns a lighter aid when he co-operates.

## 3. The horse pauses before moving forwards

There should be no delay at the end of the rein-back before moving forwards.

♦ This can be due to poor co-ordination of the aids.

♦ If the rein-back was not executed properly, he may not have engaged the hind legs, so struggles to move directly forwards.

### SOLUTIONS

**a** The rider must be mentally ready to change his aids as soon as the desired number of rein-back steps have been made.

For example, you ask for three steps back; as the horse makes the third step, bring your legs forwards to the girth, give the signal to go forwards, sit up and lighten the rein contact to allow the horse to move, whether you have chosen walk, trot or canter. If the timing of any of these aids is late, then the horse may stop before moving forwards.

**b** If the rein-back was poorly ridden and the horse was dropping his back and dragging his hooves, then this may be the cause of the delay and must be addressed in order to cure the problem.

♦ Refer to the advice above on riding the rein-back.

## 4. Horse takes too many steps backwards

Rein-back is usually for a specified number of steps (often three or four) which should be shown calmly.

♦ If the horse has been made tense, he may be anxious and run back.

♦ Occasionally he may stop listening and hurry back as an evasion.

## SOLUTIONS

**a** If he is tense, then we have to take time to re-train him and gain his trust. Ask quietly for just a single rein-back step. Be sure to praise him. The trainer can offer him a piece of sugar to encourage him not to run back.

- ◆ Repeat the process, taking care to be very calm so that your horse gains confidence. In time this will help to keep him relaxed when asked for the rein-back.

- ◆ If the horse persists in running back, then the trainer can discourage further steps by holding a lunge whip horizontally behind the horse. Note that this must be done tactfully so the horse is not frightened.

**b** If it is an evasion, then reinforce the forward impulse in your horse. Ride forwards boldly in medium trot or canter. Then halt, ask for just one step back, then forwards boldly again. As noted above, your trainer can hold the lunge whip behind the horse as a deterrent. Remember to praise him when he moves forwards

# FLYING CHANGES

See photo sequence overleaf.

- ◆ This is a change of canter lead in the air, with no trot or walk steps.

- ◆ It happens in the moment of suspension when there are no hooves on the ground.

- ◆ The changes can be single (one on its own) or tempi, that is, changing the lead every fourth, third, second or every stride.

- ◆ Any change should be straight, with no deviation of the quarters to one side or the other.

- ◆ The horse should remain on the bit.

- ◆ The canter should show lively impulsion and good balance.

- ◆ The horse should perform them calmly.

## Thoughts on flying changes

- ◆ Before attempting changes, the horse should be able to canter with collection, remaining calm, and straight and balanced.

1. The first picture shows the rider in collected canter right, preparing to ask for the flying change to the left. She has opened her outside (*left*) leg by moving it forward to the girth, but does not use it in this moment.

2. The new outside leg (*right*) has moved behind the girth to ask the horse to make the change to left lead. This fabulous picture shows the moment of suspension with all four hooves off the ground. This suspension is one of the marks of a good flying change.

3. Caroline sits still throughout, allowing an expressive change.

- He should be able to perform precise, simple changes anywhere in the school and from light aids.

- He should be secure in counter-canter and rein-back, as they are useful tools in the changes work.

## The aids for a single flying change

- Ensure the canter is on the aids, straight, balanced and with lively strides.

- A horse can change cleanly when all his hooves are briefly in the air, so your aids must have good timing and be fast, but light.

- Warn your horse by making half-halts.

- Keep even contact on the reins and stay upright in the saddle.

- To make the change, move the old outside leg forward to the girth, *but do not use it*. This is called 'opening the outside leg'.

- When you open the old outside leg, move it in the same rhythm as your horse; if it is faster or slower it will cause problems in future tempi changes.

- As you open the old outside leg, move the old inside leg back behind the girth and touch your horse. This is the signal for him to change.

- As soon as he has made the change, the new inside leg at the girth asks for a good quality canter stride and the new outside leg reverts to its normal passive state.

## SUGGESTED EXERCISES
### FOR INTRODUCING THE SINGLE FLYING CHANGE

There are many ways to ride a flying change. Here are a few suggestions.

In all the following exercises, make sure you prepare the canter so that it is collected, straight and has impulsion. Your horse needs to be responding to light aids if he is to make clean and good quality changes.

**a** We can use a small figure of eight pattern.

- For instance on the right rein, canter a 10m circle at K. A well-ridden small circle will help achieve the necessary degree of collection and balance. Riding from one small circle to another on the opposite rein is an incentive for the horse to make the flying change.

### 3. The horse changes late in front

SOLUTION

This is less common. Just before asking for the change, adjust the positioning to the new direction and then ask with the legs.

## 4. The horse swings his haunches

A correct flying change remains straight, the hind legs following the forelegs.

SOLUTIONS

**a** The rider's seat is often the cause.

- Sit still in the saddle. Twisting the upper body will frequently cause the horse to swing his haunches.

- Using the leg aids too strongly may make the haunches deviate. Remember to relax and ask with light aids. If the simple changes have been ridden correctly with light touches from the leg, then flying changes are also possible this way.

- Do not take your legs too far back; one or two hand widths behind the girth is enough. Further can make him move his hindquarters to the side.

- Using the reins too much to bend the horse in the new direction can cause it. The reins should be subtle in their application. 'Less is more' is a good guideline.

**b** If he swings the haunches inwards when trying a change on the wall, try making the change on an inside track. This often gives the rider better control of the straightness as the horse does not try to keep both his outside shoulder and hip close to the wall, creating a crooked position.

## 5. The horse speeds up after the change

The canter should remain in the same tempo, before during and after a flying change.

SOLUTIONS

**a** The rider must stay upright in the saddle. Looking down to see if the horse has changed can cause him to speed up. The horse needs the consistency of a correctly seated rider to keep his own rhythm and balance.

**b** Many horses find learning a change exciting and can buck or run off. They must be ridden tactfully.

- ◆ If you are not confident or are not practised at flying changes, ask someone who is experienced to teach the horse for you. Their skill can help the horse understand and if they can teach him without mistakes, he will become more relaxed with the changes.

- ◆ When a horse is learning the flying change, the sudden alteration in his balance can lead to speeding up. It is most important that the rider stays quiet in the saddle. If he pulls at the reins to keep his own balance, it will make the horse worry, and next time he may be worse.

- ◆ If the horse speeds up after the change, the rider can make circles and give and re-take the reins to steady the tempo and calm the horse.

- ◆ If he persists, make a calm walk transition.

- ◆ With an older horse, we can quietly halt, rein-back and then pick up the canter again. This sometimes needs to be repeated a few times to imprint good behaviour on the horse!

- ◆ Think about where to make the change; asking when close to the wall of the arena can help, rather than facing the long side with lots of space to run into.

- ◆ If the horse is inclined to buck during a change, it may help to prepare him by riding a few trot steps then ask for the new lead. In time reduce the number of trot steps and when he is doing this calmly, ask for a flying change. This is a good method for excitable horses, and may take some time to establish a calm state of mind.

## 6. The changes are short

The canter should not deteriorate as a result of the change. Look for the same length of strides from start to finish.

The causes may be related to faulty aiding or a lack of suppleness.

### SOLUTIONS

**a** The rider must remain relaxed when riding the flying changes. Horses can change easily when loose in their paddock, so keep it easy for them under saddle too.

- ◆ If we become tense in our back and hands, we affect the throughness of our horse and the changes will suffer.

- The rider should think 'forward' for every change. Over-shortening the canter in a mistaken attempt to obtain collection can stiffen the horse through his body and spoil the changes.

**b** If the canter is lacking energy, then the changes can be too short. An option is to ride medium canter across the diagonal, collect and then ask for the change. This can help to bring the hind legs through with more reach to the stride.

- Try riding the flying changes outside in a level field. This can energise the canter and produce more expressive changes.

- If the horse generally lacks suppleness or is stiff due to age, then do not ask for the changes too early in the session. Make sure you have worked him in properly so that he is loose, round and through. He must not be so tired that he has no energy for the changes, but we must give him a chance to lose any stable stiffness.

- Although the canter needs to be collected for the changes, it does not need to be at the same level as for canter pirouettes. Therefore with a stuffy or very placid horse, we can ride changes at a stronger tempo.

**c** A flying change should look equal in either direction. A lack of straightness can cause the change to be shorter in one direction. In this case we need to return to basics and work on achieving an ambidextrous horse. Lateral work and counter-canter will be very useful.

For further details, see the 'Straightness' section on page 71.

For further details, see the 'Straightness' section on page 71.

> *As ever, we want the horse to be on our aids, so he waits for our prompt…*

## 7. The horse anticipates the changes

As ever, we want the horse to be on our aids, so he waits for our prompt, rather than guesses or anticipates.

### SOLUTIONS

**a** Anticipation may happen if we repeat the change in the same place too often.

- Although it can be helpful to ask in the same place when teaching the change, it is advisable to alternate making a change with just cantering through the same place with no change. The idea is to train the horse to listen for our aid and not just to do it at a certain place in the arena.

**b** We must be careful to sit still. When we are readying ourselves to make a change, if we inadvertently move our weight, the horse will recognise this and may offer the change. He should not be punished for this; rather we must improve our seat.

- Equally, a sloppy leg position can cause a premature change. For example, if the outside leg drifts forwards instead of remaining behind the girth. This can easily be interpreted by the horse as the outside leg 'opening' prior to a flying change aid.

c With an older horse who already knows flying changes, we may need to vary our patterns to prevent anticipation.

- For example, if he has become used to changes every time he starts a long diagonal, then we must ride it with no changes and if he does one anyway, stop, and quietly ask for the old lead again. This requires patience from the rider to teach the horse to wait for the aids. It will also teach the rider to sit very still in the saddle!

# TEMPI CHANGES

- These are a series of flying changes performed after a given number of strides.
- In competition, they are every fourth, third, second or every stride.
- The number of strides in a sequence is counted when the leading foreleg touches the ground.
- Before attempting tempi changes, the horse must be absolutely secure in single flying changes, and be able to remain calm, straight, round and through.
- He must be able to do single changes anywhere in the arena with precision.
- He must be straight on both reins.

## SUGGESTED EXERCISES

- Begin with two single changes, one at either end of the long side. Imagine riding around the short end of the arena on the right rein, with inside (right) lead canter. As soon as you are straight on the long side, make a flying change to counter-canter. Maintain this until the final corner marker, then ride a flying change to the inside lead.
- Keep as calm as possible and reward his efforts with a long rein walk.

- This process can be developed over time so that you can ride the exercise on both reins, on and off the track.

- If there are mistakes, analyse what went wrong so that you do not repeat them and teach the horse the *wrong* things.

- The aim is to reduce the number of strides between changes, so that next you will fit in three changes on the long side, and on both reins.

Everyone makes mistakes. The point is to learn from them and not repeat them over and over because it can confuse and tire your horse.

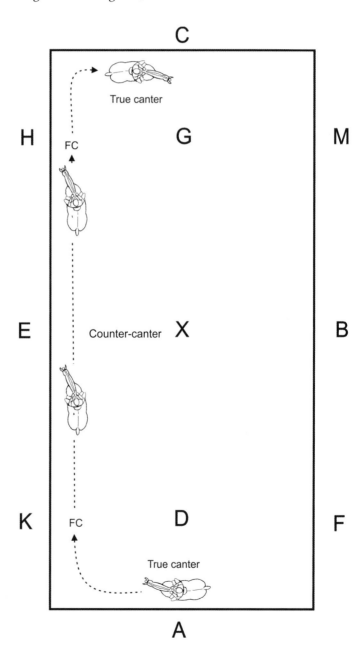

Shown here, and on pages 171–2 are three examples of how to develop from single flying changes towards tempi changes.

◆ A different method could be to ride a 5m shallow loop on the long side of the arena. At the deepest point, level with the half school marker, make a flying change to the outside lead, and then change again to the inside just before the corner. The slight change of direction can help indicate the other lead is wanted.

◆ The shallow loops can be sophisticated into shallow serpentines either side of the centre line, with a change when crossing the centre line.

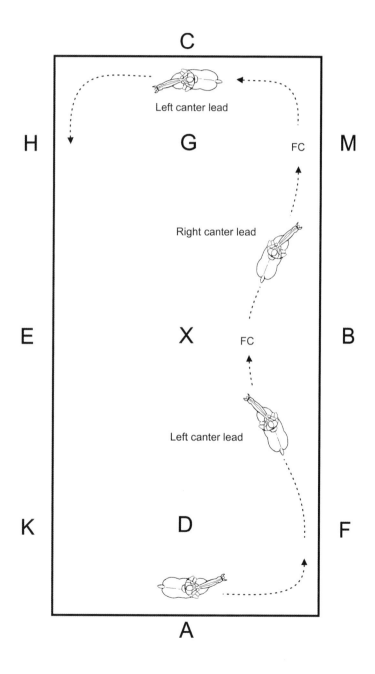

- A three-loop serpentine, with loops 2 or 3m deep, will produce two changes, whereas a four-loop serpentine will give three flying changes. The more loops, the fewer strides there will be between each change.

- Riding changes every fourth stride can be started along the wall, as this helps to prevent the horse from swinging the quarters outwards.

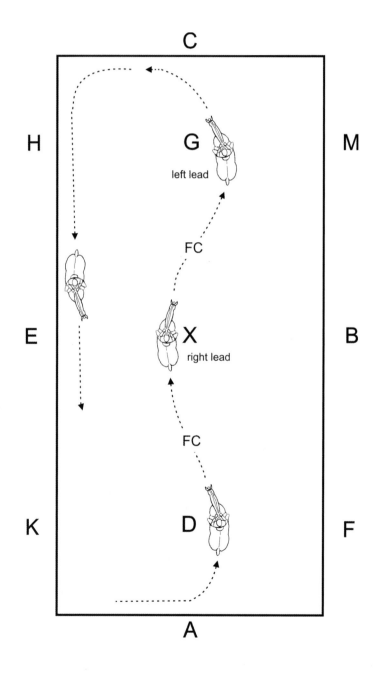

- Riding changes on a large circle is also a good exercise and some will find this easier. The circle helps to prevent the horse from swinging to one side.

- When these feel secure, try them across the diagonals. Remember to count in your head the number of strides you are aiming for, so you do not lose the sequence.

- To keep the diagonal from wavering, look through your horse's ears and keep your eyes on your destination marker. Aim for a straight horse on a straight line.

- Only when the four-time changes are safe should you progress to trying every three, then two strides. This can take several weeks.

- Whilst training the changes, have some sessions with no changes so that the horse is not pressured. Keep everything as calm and relaxed as possible.

## Changes every stride

- When the horse is confident with changes every second stride, you can try them every stride.

- The rider needs to ask for a calm yet lively collection – perhaps a little stronger than for the two-time changes.

- The horse must be straight.

- On a large circle make a flying change to counter-canter, then immediately back to inside lead. If your timing is good, most horses can manage this. Be sure to do it in both directions. Making the change from counter-canter to the inside is an inviting option and should encourage the horse to make the change.

- We must also ask the horse to do it on straight lines; for example just before a corner, change to the outside lead, then immediately back to the inside. Then ask for this in the middle of the long side.

- These must be secure before asking for three in a row. This can prove more difficult for the horse, but remain patient and when he can make three in one place, ride on then ask for three more elsewhere. When this is mastered one can gradually build to four or more changes in a row.

# PROBLEMS WITH TEMPI CHANGES

Many problems are the same as in any other change sequence, but here are some thoughts on the one-time changes.

## 1. The horse misses one or more changes

### SOLUTIONS

**a** The most likely problem is that the rider's timing was too slow.

- Remember that the aids must be *fast* – you must work *with* your horse, not behind him. Touch him with your outside leg immediately after the first change and then after every subsequent change.

- Remember to relax the leg after giving each aid otherwise the horse will feel as if it is gripping, not aiding.

- The aids must also be light and refined. For example, there is neither time to move the leg aids a long way back, nor to significantly change the flexion each stride; and if the earlier flying change work was done correctly this would be unnecessary, as the horse would be trained to listen and react to gestures which are quick and subtle.

- The rider's upper body cannot afford to swing around in the saddle, as this can disturb the horse's balance enough to miss a change.

- It is a good idea for the rider to have a clear mental picture of the one-time changes in his head before starting them, then stay focused and be alive to the feeling of what is going on underneath him.

**b** It may be that the horse is not ready for the 'one-times'.

- If there are mistakes despite the rider's timing being exact, correct back a step and try fewer one-time changes. Make sure the horse is rewarded when he offers a few correctly. Do not be in a hurry otherwise you can make him anxious and these changes can become a problem for the horse.

- A loss of balance can result in a missed change. Check that the quality of the canter is good; straight, engaged and with lively yet calm energy.

**c** If the canter is too flat and lacking in collection, then the changes may start well, but then mistakes can appear.

◆ Focus on the cadence and impulsion. Riding medium canter, then collecting and asking for the one-times can be helpful. If this is successful, it demonstrates that the canter needs improvement for the one-times to become secure.

## 2. The changes swing

There should be no deviation in the horse's body from side to side.

### SOLUTIONS

**a** The rider may be applying one leg stronger than the other, or becoming stronger on one rein.

  ◆ Refined aids are necessary at this level. The leg aids should be both light and applied an equal distance behind the girth.

◆ Although the new outside rein helps to keep the horse straight, it must not pull.

**b** The rider may be twisting his upper body during the changes, causing the horse to swing. Any body movement must be subtle, almost imperceptible.

**c** Although riding the tempi changes along the wall can help straightness, on occasion the horse may swing because he wishes to lean towards the wall. In this instance, ride on an inside track and be very even in your aiding.

> If swinging persists, revert back to working on the straightness of the canter without any flying changes.
>     Any crookedness is always obvious in canter and even more so when riding changes.

## 3. The changes are short

*Any* flying change should be big, upwards and forwards in the strides.

### SOLUTIONS

**a** Again examine the quality of the canter preceding the changes. If it is on the forehand, the changes will be short and, instead of showing expression, may be croup-high and appear to bury themselves down into the ground.

◆ Fatigue can be a cause. A horse is not a machine, so he is only capable of a certain number of changes in a session before he becomes weary. This depends on his stamina and mental relaxation. If tiredness is an issue, then the horse should not be asked for more and more changes just so the rider can practise. Leave that for another day so that next time the horse is enthusiastic and fresh.

> Over-training can be as detrimental as too little, therefore it is important that we try hard not to repeat our mistakes, otherwise we ask our horses too often and they become tired and stale.

**b** Take care not to look down. This can upset the horse's balance and rhythm. Look forward between his ears.

**c** If the horse is to maintain the quality of the changes, the rider must use the reins at a minimum; only enough contact to keep his head and neck straight. Stronger than this can shorten the changes or cause the horse to twist his neck and lose straightness.

**d** If a horse is tense, then it can make the changes short and flat. Take time to relax him, stretching him so that he can relax his back and swing once again. Then the rider can ask for a single flying change and assess its quality. Only if it is big, round and through with an uphill feel should the tempi changes be tried again that day.

# 7

# PIAFFE AND PASSAGE

## PIAFFE

### General thoughts

- Piaffe is a trot-like movement as the legs move in diagonal pairs, but *without* a moment of suspension.

- The horse will be collected and cadenced, showing even, rhythmic steps that are almost on the spot.

- The horse needs to be elastic, supple and strong, so the hind legs can show more flexion and lower the croup. This means the hindquarters carry more weight, allowing the forehand to be lighter so the front legs only lightly touch the ground.

- In an ideal piaffe, the toe of one hind leg is lifted to the height of the fetlock of the standing hind leg and the foreleg is raised so that the forearm is parallel to the ground.

- The head and neck will be arched, with a tall poll. The appearance should be of lightness, with the horse remaining on the aids.

- Although the piaffe is shown on the spot (or nearly so) he should be able to move forwards at an instant. This requires the piaffe to be springy, with a forwards quality to it.

Piaffe in double bridle.

## Introducing piaffe

◆ Piaffe is not just for advanced horses. Piaffe-like steps can be introduced to young horses as a means of teaching them how to flex their haunches, which strengthens and activates them.

◆ There are several ways of introducing piaffe work. Many prefer starting in-hand, as the horse has the chance to learn what is required without the weight of a rider on his back.

## In-hand preparation

Work in-hand is potentially a very useful aspect of training. However, it is a very skilled activity and should only be tried by experienced trainers.

Do not attempt it unless you have had some training from a knowledgeable person. Done incorrectly it can be damaging to the horse and possibly dangerous to the person.

It requires great tact, patience and the ability to 'read' the horse's body language. Timing of the aids is vital, as is the correct positioning of the trainer in relation to the horse.

- Before embarking on in-hand work, the horse should already be familiar with working in the lungeing equipment – a correctly fitted cavesson over the snaffle bridle, a saddle with lunge roller fitted over it, side reins and boots or bandages in front.

- Put the tail up with a bandage over it so that the quarters are free to be touched with the whip.

- Working in-hand is best practised in an enclosed arena for safety, plus the walls can help to keep the horse straight.

- Before you begin, take as much time as necessary to accustom him to being touched with the piaffe whip on his hind legs, croup and over his neck and back. The piaffe whip is used as an aid, not a punishment, so he must learn to trust the trainer.

- Take time and watch your horse. Only if is he is calm should you proceed quietly to the next step. A tense horse can be difficult to manage and lead to difficulties in the work.

- In-hand work is best introduced with an assistant. The helper will have the lead rein, attached to the centre ring of the cavesson. The trainer with the piaffe whip will then be positioned so that he can touch the haunches. The trainer will give the instructions, but it must be teamwork.

- The side reins are attached to the lunge roller. They should be of equal length and bring the horse onto the bit with his nose just in front of the vertical but not behind it.

- Both trainer and assistant are positioned to the horse's inside.

- Many horses find it easier to begin on the left rein. If there is an assistant, he will lead the horse to a square halt on the track. The wall helps to keep him straight.

- The trainer then softly touches the inside hind leg to ask the horse to calmly raise that leg. When he does, be sure to praise him.

> *A tense horse can be difficult to manage and lead to difficulties in the work.*

# Developing the piaffe

♦ When the horse understands the piaffe in-hand, it is time to try it under a rider.

♦ This may begin as a development from the in-hand work.

♦ The rider is the number one in the team. The horse must now learn the piaffe aids from his rider and not rely on the person on the ground.

♦ The trainer is there to support; he is the number two in this situation. Rider and trainer need to be experienced and have good feel if the horse is to stay relaxed.

♦ The rider works the horse in until he is ready to offer collection.

♦ A correct piaffe demonstrates good balance and strength so should only be attempted when the horse is capable of taking weight back onto his haunches.

♦ From collected walk beside the arena wall, ask for a few piaffe-like steps. (half-steps) allowing the horse to move a little forwards. This is both to keep the horse forward-thinking and to avoid tension, which could happen if too much is demanded too soon.

♦ If the horse does not understand the rider's aids, then the trainer can use the piaffe whip to touch the hind legs alternately, in the correct rhythm. Do not use the whip faster than the horse moves.

♦ Piaffe takes time to develop until it gradually becomes more in place. Rushing this can lead to tension, loss of balance and rhythm.

♦ When the horse offers a few piaffe steps (three or four will be enough at the start) then be sure to stop and pat him to let him know you are pleased with his efforts.

♦ When the horse understands what is required, it is a good idea to follow the piaffe steps with some collected trot to refresh the impulsion – we do not want stopping to become a habit.

♦ As always, we should keep our horse straight and practise on both reins evenly.

♦ A good exercise to develop the horse is to ride collected trot, then very collected for a few steps only, then forward into collection again. It is most important to keep the diagonal rhythm when making the very collected steps and that we can keep the horse very round over his back.

♦ In the piaffe, the horse should really sit and lower the haunches to show collection. If you stand behind him and can see the whole sole of the hind hoof, then he is not collected enough, it is merely a short diagonal stride.

+ At the end of the session, we should allow the horse to relax on a long rein before returning to his stable. We want the horse to enjoy this work too.

*After a training session, it is good to allow the horse to relax mentally and physically. He reaches politely forwards and downwards when a longer rein is offered and swings through the back.*

## PROBLEMS WITH PIAFFE

+ Moving backwards, irregular steps with the hind legs, crossing either the fore or hind legs, are bad faults.

+ Swinging either the forehand or the quarters from side to side are also serious errors.

+ A movement with hurried steps without cadence or spring cannot be called a true piaffe. It is merely stamping or fidgeting.

+ Leaning stiffly onto the forehand rather than raising it is a fault.

### SOLUTIONS

+ The trainer should consider whether the horse was actually ready for this very demanding, collected work. If the horse has not the strength in his haunches, he cannot make a correct piaffe; and if forced to continue, it will produce some of the faults listed above.

- Only when the haunches have been strengthened enough to take weight back and remain supple and elastic is he ready to try piaffe again.

- Rocking from side to side is often the result of a lack of balance or stiffness, leading to the horse trying to lean on his forelegs alternately. Assess the horse's suppleness. Make sure that you are giving him the chance to work properly by thoroughly warming him up before attempting piaffe.

- Some riders apply the leg aids alternately. This can cause swinging. Use the legs at the same time and in rhythm.

- If the forelegs are brought back under the horse rather than straight down, or if the hind legs step too far forwards, then balance will be lost. In the latter case it becomes difficult to raise the hind legs and the forehand lifts too much. Improve the situation by riding some active transitions to preserve the forward impulse.

- If the horse is stiff in his back, or weak in his haunches, then the rhythm will be lost and the croup may bounce upwards and the forelegs appear to be stuck to the ground. Try riding rein-back then piaffe. This should lift the back and by loosening the back muscles, help to make the rhythm more even.

- These problems have their origin in lack of suppleness. Therefore try riding many transitions between medium and collected trot or canter to check that the horse is genuinely on the aids and is through his body.

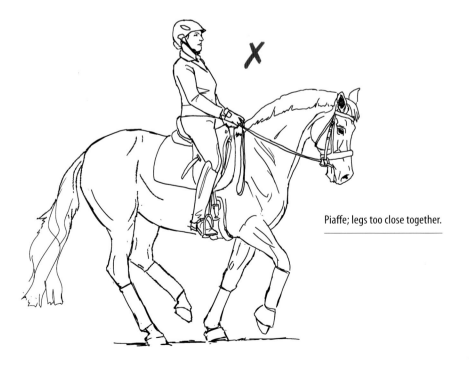

Piaffe; legs too close together.

- Sometimes the rider's seat may be to blame. If he cannot sit still he will disturb the horse's balance, or if he pulls on the reins instead of sitting into his horse, it will create stiffness and tension.

- Some people are happy if the horse just shows some diagonal movement; but this is not enough to be called piaffe. It must be very collected; seated in the haunches with the weight back.

If the horse is not supple or strong in his back, he cannot lower the haunches and, if asked for piaffe, will respond by leaning on the forehand and bouncing his croup upwards.

If the horse is stiff in his back, or weak in his haunches, then the rhythm will be lost.

- If the piaffe is uneven, then work on making the weaker leg stronger. Lateral work will help develop the overall strength and suppleness.

- Using cavalletti is an option, as is riding up and down hills in the countryside. Incorporating this into his conditioning work can be fun for your horse and is a good way of keeping him fresh.

# PASSAGE

## General thoughts

- This is a collected, very suspended and cadenced trot.

- It requires a pronounced engagement of the quarters, a noticeable flexion of the knees and hocks, and should look graceful and elastic.

- It can be trained from piaffe, trot, half-steps or the walk.

- The horse must be very straight and very through his back.

- When both horse and rider can display excellent balance, the passage gives the impression of floating.

> *The feeling is one of slow but majestic steps, that spring up and forwards.*

## Developing passage

- Piaffe is often taught before passage; but if the horse lacks impulsion, it may be better to teach passage first, as this tends to increase the energy.

- A correct passage is developed from forward movement, not by holding back the horse.

- The rider can ride many transitions, including from medium or extended work to collection. These transitions must be totally straight, through the back and promptly on the rider's aids. If this is not possible, then the horse is not ready.

## Aids for passage

- To be clear, before asking for passage, the horse must be straight, engaged, through his back and strong in his muscles.

- The rider's legs ask for more impulsion with pushing aids.

- The seat and back muscles tone up to contain the extra impulsion created. The aim is for upward, floating steps, not faster and flatter ones.

- The hands allow the horse to move slightly forward at each step. The feeling is one of slow but majestic steps, that spring up and forwards.

## From trot

- Ride many transitions within the trot. The horse must be thoroughly on the aids and able to go from collected to extended trot in an instant.

- Gradually make these transitions more frequent to assess his balance and obedience.

- From collected trot, use half-halts to bring the horse very collected, at the same time asking for more impulsion with the legs. The seat is firmed up to contain the forward element of the stride and the reins allow the horse a little forward so that the steps become more elevated and suspended.

- In essence it is a transition from collected to extended trot, with the rider using seat and rein aids to check the extended stride the moment it is offered, creating an upward, forward and floating feeling.

- The main difference between the trot aids and those for the passage is the extra amount of seat required for passage. In turn this calls for the rider to have a deep independent seat so that he does not disturb the horse at a critical moment.

- Ask for only a few steps then walk and praise the horse. Do not tire him or he may resent the work next time.

## From piaffe

- When teaching passage from piaffe, this too can be introduced from the ground.

- The balance and engagement needed for piaffe are also required for passage.

- When the piaffe is established in-hand, we can ask the horse to move more forward, allowing him to show the elevated passage steps.

- After he offers some passage, allow the horse to trot forwards. Do not over-tax his mind or body. He needs time to absorb new lessons.

- When progressing to teach passage under saddle, help from the ground is again recommended. The trainer is there to confirm the rider's aids if needed, but the idea is that the horse learns the aids from seat, legs and reins. It can be helpful if the trainer touches the forelegs lightly with the whip if they are not lifting sufficiently. At no time should this become harsh. The idea is to give light touches, not to hurt or frighten the horse.

◆ The rider's legs increase the forward-driving aids yet taking care not to push the horse out of rhythm. The reins allow the horse to move a little forward.

◆ The upper body must remain very still (that is, from the middle of the back to the top of the head) yet show an increased swing in the lower back to absorb the extra motion.

◆ After riding a handful of passage steps, walk on a long rein to reward and relax the horse.

## From walk

◆ Walk often has less impulsion than trot or piaffe, making it difficult to teach the passage, but has the advantage that it is easier for the rider to learn to apply his aids because the walk is smoother.

◆ If the horse is inclined to speed up in the piaffe to passage transition, then teaching from walk or trot may be tried.

◆ The aids for the passage will be the same from the rider.

◆ The method chosen really depends on watching and knowing your horse. Pick the easiest way depending on his temperament and conformation.

# PROBLEMS WITH PASSAGE

## 1. The horse offers passage, but he is stiff in his neck and back

### SOLUTION

◆ If the rider is too strong in his hands, it can cause the head to lift up and the back to drop and hollow. The rider needs to improve the depth and suppleness of his seat, so he can remain in harmony with the horse during passage. Otherwise he will be balancing on the reins, preventing the horse from swinging in his back.

## 2. The horse leans on the reins

SOLUTION

◆ The reins may be too short, leading to the horse lying on the reins or even trying to run away from the pressure. The correct outline is achieved by closing the horse from the haunches forwards towards the bridle, not by manipulating the head and neck into a short, constrained position.

◆ If the horse speeds up when the reins are lengthened little, we may conclude the rider does not have the horse sufficiently on the seat aids. Remembering the truism that 'we should not push more than we can control with our seat,' the rider must work on his seat until he can sit deeply enough to 'hold' the horse with his abdominal and back muscles rather than the hands. It is important to realise that the back must not become rigid when practising this, but should remain flexible.

## 3. The hind legs take uneven steps

SOLUTIONS

◆ This may be due to the rider applying his legs unevenly. He may need to use his leg more effectively, or support it with a tap from the whip, on the side which takes the shorter hind leg step.

◆ Try to ride the horse more positively forward. Be aware of the feeling of his hind legs; do they work equally underneath you, or does one of your seat bones get moved less than the other?

◆ Alternatively, the uneven steps can be the result of crookedness in the horse. If so, this must be rectified before proceeding with further passage work.

◆ Working the passage in-hand can help the horse find and keep the rhythm better. The cavesson and side reins offer a consistent contact, and without the weight of the rider he may find it easier to show a good quality-passage. Work in piaffe before the passage to improve engagement and activity.

## 4. The hind legs drag

This would indicate a lack of balance, probably due to insufficient impulsion. The energy must be freshened up by riding energetic transitions.

SOLUTION

♦ A helpful exercise is to ride extended canter down the long side of the arena, then make a transition into passage as soon as possible, so the horse is energised from the extension, creating more lift in the hind legs.

♦ It will also help to ride him in collected trot and to make many transitions. The idea is to activate the hind legs, a necessity for passage.

♦ A horse who drags or leaves his hind legs out behind rather engaging them under his body, may be stiff in the back due to strong rein contact (see above) or it may be partly a conformation fault. A horse with a long back or with his hocks built out behind will find passage difficult. He needs careful training to strengthen his body and to help him learn to lift his back and tuck his pelvis so that he can engage correctly. During passage the horse's back muscles must contract and release to the utmost and this can only happen if he has strength and suppleness.

## 5. The horse offers passage with a tense back

SOLUTION

♦ This can be caused by rushing the training and pursuing the passage before the horse is physically ready. If this problem appears at an early stage, the rider can correct it by riding more forwards into medium or extended trot, or asking for lateral exercises in collected trot.

♦ However if the fault has become established, it can be very difficult to cure.

♦ One sometimes sees this fault in sports horses who have been bred with very big movement. Some people may try to exploit this by pushing for the passage because the trot has a 'passage' quality about it naturally. However, unless the horse's body and mind have been properly prepared over time, this can lead to a false passage where only the legs move but the body is held stiffly, this being the only way the horse can show what is being asked of him.

## 6. I ask for passage, but the horse offers a faster trot

This can be because the horse lacks impulsion in his haunches.

SOLUTIONS

♦ If the passage is being attempted from the piaffe, we can try it from the walk or trot instead. We must see whether the horse finds this an easier way.

♦ It may be that the horse needs more time to perfect the piaffe enough to show the necessary level of collection and engagement for the passage.

## 7. The passage rocks or the forelegs cross

Both of these are serious faults.

### SOLUTIONS

♦ The root of the problem may lie in body stiffness. A horse who is asked for passage can rock to compensate for the stiffness in his hips. If this is not corrected it may lead to the forelegs crossing over.

♦ The answer is to really take care to loosen the horse thoroughly before working on the passage.

♦ Once again we must be aware of balance between horse and rider. Unless this is very good, the quality of the passage will be affected.

## Concluding thoughts on piaffe/passage problems

In all the examples we have looked at, we are thinking about the horse or rider learning the piaffe/passage. However, in many cases it happens that the rider has bought an older schoolmaster horse who knows the movements and this of course can be tremendously valuable.

Nonetheless, sometimes through age or perhaps faulty training in the past, the horse performs the movements incorrectly. If the faults are long standing, or if through age a horse is no longer as supple as he once was, then it may be that despite our best efforts, we cannot correct everything.

Naturally we will continue to follow correct training principles and try to make our horse as comfortable as possible and learn from what our schoolmaster can teach us.

If the horse is still fit enough to compete, then we must also accept that he may not score well in certain movements, but regard it as a valuable learning opportunity for ourselves.

At all times we must consider the horse's well-being before our own, but also be aware that we can learn much from the 'professors'.

> *At all times we must consider the horse's well-being before our own.*

191

And finally...

# 8

# THE
# HIGH SCHOOL
# JUMPS

The 'airs above the ground' as practised in the Spanish Riding School, are first taught in-hand, although this is not the only way to start the exercises. They were regarded as the peak of dressage training, demonstrating complete trust between horse and rider as well as the horse's power, courage and ability. They are not part of the FEI dressage tests and are performed correctly in only a few establishments around the world. Our pictures are from the Classical Riding School at the Lipica Stud Farm in Slovenia.

*Only very knowledgeable, experienced trainers* should consider  teaching the High School jumps, as it takes great understanding to gauge whether a horse has the talent, temperament and power to do the Airs. The rider must also have courage and an impeccable seat. To attempt the work without these qualities would be a disaster.

Few breeds of horse can attain the levels of strength and calmness required for the High School work. This is why the Lipizzaner and the Iberian horse are the most appropriate for the Airs above the Ground. Even then, only some would be suitable for this demanding work. The trainer should only proceed if the horse is both unafraid and strong enough in his body.

The piaffe is the basis for the jumps, as when it is shown correctly the horse will be seated on the haunches displaying strength, balance, engagement and calmness of the highest order.

In this piaffe shown side-saddle, note Kristina Umek's elegant position and soft rein contact, helping Favoury Montearua to produce lively yet calm steps.

Miro Dragic with Neapolitano Strana. The connection between horse and trainer is evident from the lightness of the aids, which here produce good piaffe steps on the long reins.

# THE LEVADE

This was introduced in the nineteenth century. Prior to that, Riding Masters used the pesade as the introduction to the school jumps.

In levade, the horse bends his hocks to lower the haunches and lifts his forehand so that his body is at an angle of about 30 degrees to the ground.

Alojz Lah's exemplary seat allows Conversano Allegra to maintain deeply flexed hind legs in perfect balance. Note that the hock joints are very close to the ground, demonstrating great strength in the haunches.

Levade is often taught from the ground so that the horse can understand and find his balance without the weight of a rider.

195

The levade is the most collected exercise, with or without a rider. This is the proof that collection is about taking weight on the hindquarters, not just making short steps.

Levade is the most difficult of the High School movements because the horse must remain very calm during the challenges to his strength and balance.

When taught in-hand, the horse is brought into piaffe, and then gradually asked to become more active in place. Then the horse is asked to raise his forehand. The forelegs should be neatly tucked up and not left hanging down.

The horse should not move backwards but maintain his position for a few seconds until the trainer ends the exercise. This is demanding work for the horse, so the levade is practised sparingly.

At the end, the horse should lower his forehand to the ground lightly and be ready to move forward if asked.

During a ridden levade, the rider's upper body should remain vertical to the ground.

# PESADE

The horse raises his forehand to 45 degrees and although the hocks are bent and weight is carried on the haunches, it is not to the same degree as the levade; therefore it is a less difficult movement.

Before the introduction of the levade, pesade was the preparation for the High School jumps and Airs above the Ground.

The pesade is good preparation for the courbette (see page 198) as it will strengthen the horse's hindquarters.

The trainer must assess whether the horse has the power and balance to progress to the courbette; but also that the horse enjoys the work and is never afraid.

Note that if the horse lifts himself more than the 45 degrees of the pesade with straight hind legs, it is a rear and not a Classical movement at all.

# CAPRIOLE

The capriole is a horizontal jump, followed by both hind legs kicking backwards simultaneously, at the highest point of the jump. The capriole demands explosive power from the horse to kick out with the hind legs when he is at the maximum height of his horizontal leap, landing on all four legs very close to his point of take off.

In these two pictures, Kristina Umek and Favoury Monteaura demonstrate the pesade. Compare with the levade; here the haunches are less deeply flexed and the angle to the ground is greater. To show pesade side-saddle demonstrates the rider's great skill and empathy.

This spectacular photo captures Kristina Umek displaying the capriole in-hand, with Conversano Samira's hind legs at full extension.

When shown under saddle, the rider must have great balance, because if he were to try to balance himself with the reins instead of his seat, he could cause the horse's head to lift and result in him dropping his back and losing balance.

## COURBETTE

In the courbette, the horse makes a number of jumps, normally from two to five, on the hind legs, without the front legs touching the ground. Both hind legs should jump together, requiring great strength.

The trainer calls for an energetic piaffe, gradually bringing the horse onto the spot. Then the levade is asked for. When the levade is established, the trainer asks for a single jump with a click of the tongue and perhaps a touch from the whip on the hind legs. The horse should land on his hind legs, finishing in the levade position until touching the ground with his forelegs.

Further jumps should only be attempted when the horse is performing the courbette with confidence and understands fully what is required of him.

*opposite* Miran Mavec and Gregor Lisjak showing courbette. A wonderful picture showing Maestoso Gratiosa in mid-jump. Note the evenness of the hind legs, essential to a correct execution of the courbette.

At all times we must take care that our horses
have fun and are happy and relaxed in their work.

# CLOSING THOUGHTS

The training of horses is simple in principle; the maxim of 'Ride your horse forward and make him straight,' often attributed to General L'Hotte, encapsulates much which is essential in dressage.

However, executing these principles can prove challenging. Training is the coming together of two imperfect beings, a horse and a rider: three if we include the trainer. For a successful partnership, the humans need to be working on the same wavelength, so that the horse is educated in a logical, kind and patient manner. If not, he is likely to become confused and this can lead to problems.

To achieve this harmony, both rider and trainer need to have a clear understanding of training goals, and to have a realistic view of the time it may take to reach these goals, whilst keeping the horse's well-being at heart.

For trainers who have yet to acquire long experience, it is important to keep studying the subject, to acquire a clear grip of the theory. Whilst it is true that one cannot learn to ride well from books alone, it is equally true that without study, one cannot achieve sophistication.

During a lesson, a trainer may be presented with a number of faults to deal with. The ability to prioritise the problems and have the knowledge of how to deal with the most important one first is crucial. This is where sound judgement backed up by knowledge will ensure that steady improvements over time can be maintained.

It is important for the trainer to have an image in his mind of the finished article and that his choice of exercises and corrections is always moving towards this ideal. The ability to see 'the big picture,' but to also have the knowledge and communication skills to attend to the details is the mark of a good trainer.

As riders we also have a duty to try our best to execute what the trainer is advising. This means that we practise any homework that has been set between lessons, so that good habits are formed through continuity. Although attaining perfection may not be possible, working to achieve excellence should be every rider's goal.

Faults in the seat are often the root of problems in dressage and to neglect them is a big mistake. If the rider cannot use his seat, weight, leg and rein aids properly, how is the horse to understand and move with the freedom and grace that we seek?

In today's world, there are many sport horses that have been bred with amazing movement, far more athletic than in years gone by; but has the standard of riding risen to match these equine athletes? In some cases yes, but too often faulty training is evident or short cuts have been taken and we may see piaffe that is on the shoulder rather than sitting on the haunches, or huge trot steps from a horse with a tight back and short neck, producing spectacular leg work but not through the body.

In essence there is no conflict between competition riding and the Classical method. If we train our horses correctly, they can look beautiful both in their movement and in the quiet harmony between horse and rider, both supple and focussed. As far as we can tell, horses feel joy in moving, as we can observe when they are loose in the paddock. Our riding should enable them to express that joy.

# GLOSSARY

**Blueprint** Term used to denote the ideal template for a movement or the rider's position.

**Cavalletti** Small jumps created by fixing wooden rails to a cross piece at each end, allowing three different heights. Used in gymnastic exercises to improve the horse's suppleness and strength.

**Collection** One of the gait variations. Achieving collection is a long-term process and is evident when the horse is sufficiently strong and supple in his hindquarters to carry more of his body weight on the haunches. This shift in weight and balance lightens the forehand and allows greater manoeuvrability. Correctly ridden, piaffe and levade may be regarded as the pinnacle of collection. In simple terms, the attainment of collection is the goal of dressage, as it implies the horse is strong, balanced and supple.

**Demi-volte** A volte is a 6m diameter circle, the smallest we ask the horse to perform. Thus a demi-volte is half a 6m circle.

**Engagement** A desirable quality of the hind legs. A horse is said to be engaged when the joints of the hind legs flex sufficiently for the hoof of each hind leg to be placed on the ground far enough forward under the belly of the horse, so that he steps under the centre of gravity. This also implies that the back is supple enough to lift upwards, allowing the horse's pelvis to tuck and for the hind limb to reach further forwards. An engaged horse is capable of moving with lift and suspension, rather than just forwards propulsion.

**Extension** One of the gait variations. A horse is extended when his stride is at the maximum length he is capable of, *without* compromising his balance, rhythm or outline. It requires a demanding level of strength and suppleness, hence is not required of novice horses.

**Flying change** A change of canter lead (e.g. from right to left or vice versa) in the moment when all the horse's hooves are in the air. If the hind legs change after the front legs, the change is said to be *late behind,* or if the front legs change after the hind legs (less common) the change is said to be *late in front.*

**Half-pass** A lateral movement in which the horse moves both forwards and sideways on a diagonal line, bent in the direction of travel around the rider's inside leg. The forehand should be slightly in advance of the haunches. It can be performed in walk, trot and canter. In walk and trot the outside legs should cross in front of the inside legs, whereas in canter the legs do not cross, rather the horse bounds forwards and sideways.

**Hand work** Working a horse with the trainer on foot. He may have an assistant or work alone. The horse normally is wearing a cavesson noseband, lunge line, roller and side reins, plus boots on the front legs. The trainer uses his voice, a piaffe whip and his body positioning during the training. Great skill and understanding are required to do this well.

**Impulsion** The controlled energy of the haunches that is moderated by the rider's aids. A horse travelling at maximum gallop is not showing impulsion – that is speed and the two must not be confused.

**Inside** Usually refers to the concave side of the horse when he is bending and to the rider's aids on that side. (As in 'inside rein aid'.)

It can also mean to ride the horse 1 or 2m in from the outside track of the arena, as in 'ride shoulder-in on an inside track'.

**Lateral movement** An exercise when the horse moves with both forwards and sideways steps. They supple and strengthen certain limbs and joints in the horse, and also help the rider to gain full control of all areas of the horse's body. Also known as 'two-track' work, because the forelegs and hind legs make separate paths on the ground.

**Leg-yielding** A simple lateral movement where the horse moves forwards and sideways away from the rider's inside leg aid. The horse should remain almost straight, with just a slight amount of flexion away from the direction of travel. The inside legs should cross in front of the outside ones. Leg-yielding does not require engagement, so is often the first lateral movement taught after turn on the forehand.

**Medium** One of the gait variants of walk, trot and canter.

Medium trot or canter refers to a medium amount of extension to the length of the horse's stride, between working and extended. It will show greater energy than working paces, but retain balance, roundness and throughness.

Medium walk is the everyday variety of walk, denoting that the hind hooves step at least one horseshoe length beyond the front hoofprint. It replaced the 'ordinary walk' some years ago, as medium was seen to show more energy and purpose, so encouraging a forward state of mind.

**On the aids** This term describes the physical and mental readiness of the horse to react promptly to subtle aiding from the rider. Similar to the German '*durchlaessigkeit,*' a horse that is on the aids will be relaxed physically so that tension does not inhibit his ability to swing through a lifting back, so that the energy from the haunches is not blocked, allowing the horse to move with suspension in trot and canter. The horse will also be mentally relaxed and show willing obedience to the rider's wishes.

**Outside** Refers to the convex side of the horse's body when bending and to the rider's aids on that side.

**Pirouette** A lateral movement of collected walk or collected canter, or in piaffe, where the horse describes a full circle, with an inside bend through his body. The hind legs describe a very small circle and the forelegs a larger one. The radius of the circle should ideally be only slightly longer than the horse's body and the rhythm of the pace should be maintained during the pirouette. Can also be shown as 'half' or 'quarter' pirouettes.

**Renvers** Also known as 'tail to the wall' or 'haunches-out'. A lateral movement where the hind legs remain at the track whilst the forehand is brought inwards. The horse is bent around the rider's inside leg and looks in the direction of movement.

**Shoulder-in** A lateral movement where the rider brings the forehand of the horse a little in from the outside track, whilst the hind legs remain at the track. The horse shows a uniform bend from tail to poll around the inside leg. The purpose is to improve balance, suppleness and the engagement of the inside hind leg. It also gives the rider the ability to straighten the horse by gaining control of the placement of the forehand.

If the horse moves at an angle to the wall but has no bend, it is a leg-yield, not a shoulder-in. Shoulder-in is performed on three lines for competition, but can be on four lines in training, if the horse is supple enough. Each line represents the line of travel of each hoof or pair of hooves. Thus during shoulder-in on three lines, the outside hind is one line, the inside hind and outside foreleg together make the second line and the inside foreleg is the third line.

**Simple change**  A change of canter lead through three or four walk steps. The ability to show polished simple changes is one of the prerequisites of starting flying changes.

**Suspension**  Suspension is not present in walk, as there is always at least one hoof on the ground. In trot and canter it is desirable as it gives lift and life to the paces. It is the moment when the horse floats, with no hooves touching the ground. Suspension indicates that the horse is balanced and elastic in his joints, allowing him to spring upwards and forwards as he covers the ground. A correct passage shows the ultimate suspension.

**Tempi changes**  Riding a series of flying changes after a regular prescribed number of strides, such as 'flying change every two strides' or 'every three strides' etc.

**Transition**  The moving from one gait to another, either upwards or downwards. They may be progressive such as walk to trot, or direct (acute) e.g. canter to walk.

Transitions may also be within a gait, changing from one variation to another, such as working trot to medium, or medium canter to collected canter.

Correctly ridden transitions may be seen as the building blocks of suppleness and obedience to the aids.

**Travers**  Also known as haunches-in, this is a lateral movement where the rider brings the hindquarters in from the track, whilst the forelegs remain at the track. There is a uniform bend from tail to poll around the inside leg. The horse bends in the direction of movement. It is usually ridden on four lines.

**Turn on the forehand**  The horse turns his hindquarters around the forehand, with the inside foreleg acting as a pivot. The inside hind leg should cross in front of the outside hind. Often used as an introduction to lateral work, to teach horse or rider the basics principle of moving away from a leg aid.

# INDEX